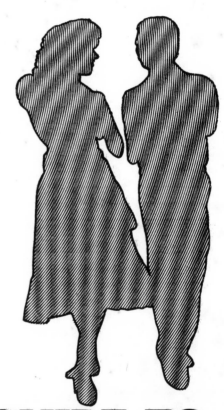

THE COMPLETE GUIDE TO
TOUCH DANCING

THE COMP

TOUCH

by

Photography by
Chart Illustrations by
Dress Designs by

ETE GUIDE TO
DANCING
Karen Lustgarten

Bernie Lustgarten
Robert Makohin and David Gentry
Gilda Forster

WARNER BOOKS

Dedicated with love to Ivan the Terrific

THE COMPLETE GUIDE TO
TOUCH DANCING

WARNER BOOKS EDITION

Designed by Thomas Nozkowski

Warner Books, Inc., 75 Rockefeller Plaza, New York, N.Y. 10019

A Warner Communications Company

Printed in the United States of America

First Printing: November, 1979

10 9 8 7 6 5 4 3 2 1

Library of Congress Cataloging in Publication Data

Lustgarten, Karen.
  The complete guide to touch dancing.

  1. Ballroom dancing. I.   Lustgarten, Bernie.
II. Title.
GV1751.L8   793.3'3   79-15635
ISBN 0-446-97218-5

ACKNOWLEDGMENTS

It's a rare pleasure to work with a man who knows how to combine his brains and talent to create beauty. I thank Bernie Lustgarten, my former husband, good friend, and understanding co-worker, for his consistently beautiful photography!

It's also a rare pleasure to have not one but *three* handsome partners join me for a second go-around. Thanks to Ivan Ladizinsky for his romantic partnering; to Dr. Robert Illa for bringing out the hot Latin side; and to Sonny Harper for being a disco daredevil with me.

Appreciation to Robert Ickes, disco dance colleague, for sharing some of his secrets on lifts, dips, and the simple Latin Hustle.

Special thanks to hair stylist Lee Bledsoe of Mister Lee of San Francisco for his wonderful styling and hair care.

My appreciation to dress designer Gilda Forster at Gilda of San Francisco for lending me her beautiful dresses for the tea and Latin dances.

Thanks to Roos-Atkins, Hillsdale, for the loan of my partner's wardrobe in Chapter Three.

Last, but not least, I'm indebted to my dear parents, who never sit still when the music plays!

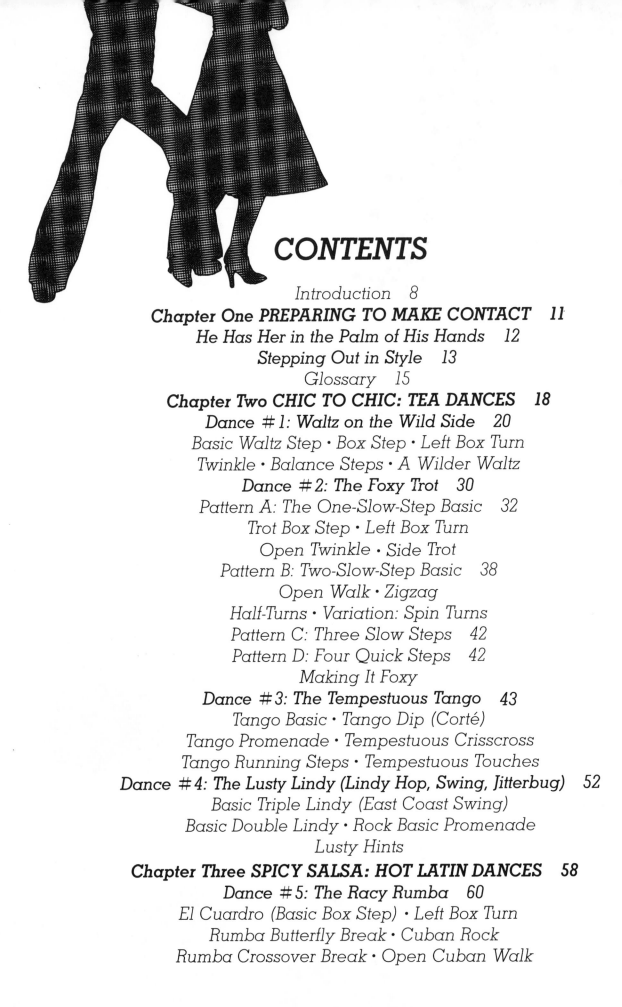

CONTENTS

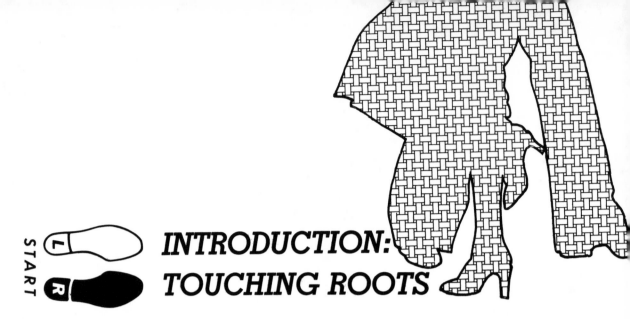

INTRODUCTION: TOUCHING ROOTS

Birds do it, bees do it, all human beings do it. We don't all necessarily touch while we're doing it, we don't all have the same reasons for doing it, but *all* living things dance. Whether it's out of instinct, ritual, celebration, or recreation, dance is a universal form of communication.

Partner dancing as we know and love it has a remarkably long and tenacious history. Before the twelfth century, recreational dancing was mainly a group affair with everyone linking hands to form long chain lines and circles. The first real couple dance to debut was the Estampie. It was nothing to get excited about, just a slow, stately court dance with simple gliding steps, but it did prepare the way for future twosomes.

When partner dances began to develop in the European courts of the thirteenth century, they were reflections of a romantic era marked by chivalrous knights in shining armor and virginal maidens left in waiting. These dignified court dances were characterized by precise, delicate steps, slow turns, and stately bows—not exactly your everyday soul dancing. By the time an Italian handbook on social dancing was written in the fifteenth century, ballroom dancing was in full bloom throughout the courts of Europe.

Seventeenth-century France under Louis XIV was a time of elaborate balls at the sumptuous palace of Versailles. Aristocrats and courtiers took lessons in the latest processional partner dances, which were something like marches. The Minuet was one of the more popular. Most of the steps in these court dances were borrowed freely from the uninhibited styles of the peasants, then tamed and formalized for the respectable royal ballrooms. Polite people danced with constraint; dancing too well or too wildly, like the peasants or lowly court entertainers, was considered barbaric.

Ballroom dancing filled the aristocrats' need to strut their stuff in an exclusive and prestigious setting. Where else could they flaunt their ostentatious clothes, affect artificial manners, and gossip? Ballrooms became the hot night spots of the aristocracy.

The history of touch dancing is really a study in sociology, since variations in dance styles reflect changes in attitudes, customs, fashion, and music. Dance is a true sign of the times. The Minuet was a reflection of Baroque dress, manners, and music. When fashion became less formal, materials softer, and hairstyles more natural, the dances became freer. The speedy turns and quick tempo of a nineteenth-century Waltz would have been difficult to accomplish in a seventeenth-century powdered wig and elaborate Baroque attire—as difficult as a corset and hooped skirt trying to make it with a stuffed shirt and tails on the disco floor.

When the Waltz arrived in the eighteenth century, there were rumblings of change in fashion and social structure. Rigid class boundaries were slowly crumbling as the royal court began to lose its control

INTRODUCTION

over the working class. Discontented nonconformists and individualists were rebelliously flaunting court styles of fashion and dancing. By the nineteenth century, the Waltz was the favorite dance of commoners and aristocrats alike.

In the late nineteenth century, the class structure really began to disintegrate, and dance hall doors were opened to the general public. Wild and crazy free-style dances developed (to be revived in the 1960s). They were performed to the black ragtime and jazz rhythms popular at the turn of the century. Everyone was letting it all hang out! The Charleston and Jitterbug are reflections of that rebellious, raucous era.

By the time soul dancing hit the sixties (preceded by rock and roll in the fifties), unisex dancers were seen in unisex clothes. Chivalry was dead. Besides, independent women didn't want to be led by men, not even on a dance floor.

The disco phenomenon of the seventies has added new and dynamic dimensions to ballroom dancing; the decade of the eighties promises a worldwide dance renaissance. Variety is the key to contemporary dance. Formal tea dancing, hot Latin, Touch Hustles, and free-style disco all comfortably coexist, and will surely narrow the generation gap.

I recommend disco dancing to senior citizens as exercise; I notice youth rediscovering touching by incorporating ballroom technique, and *everyone* seems to be out there dancing! Contemporary dance is more than mere recreation or communication; it is an exuberant celebration of life. Think of touch dancing as a *shared* expression of celebration.

CHAPTER ONE

PREPARING TO MAKE CONTACT

"Can you really teach someone with two left feet how to dance?" In the years I've been teaching disco and touch dancing, I have been asked that question countless times. Yes, I have witnessed my students convert one rejected, mislabeled left foot into a fully functioning right one, before their very eyes.

If you can walk and chew gum at the same time, you can learn to dance. If you instinctively tap your feet, sway your body, or bop your head to an irresistible beat, then you're a ripe dancing candidate. As long as you feel rhythm and have some semblance of coordination, you can dance. How quickly you learn is contingent on the quality of your instruction and practice. If the instruction is top quality, you'll look like an experienced dancer within an hour or two, and that's no exaggeration!

In this book I've given you absolutely everything you need to learn (or review) the most popular touch dances: text, foot charts, rhythm charts, photos, and recommended practice music for each dance. If foot charts confuse you, then the text, rhythm charts, and photos will clarify. If text bogs you down, then the foot charts, photos, and recommended practice music will clarify. I've organized and written this book in the easiest way possible so that *anyone* can successfully learn touch dancing. You can't lose!

There are a few pointers we should discuss before you take your first steps. Notice that each dance has its own rhythm of "slows" and "quicks." You'll save hours of frustration to your feet if your mind initially understands the counts. So be sure to learn the basic rhythms first.

After you've got the counts down, practice each step pattern separately, without a partner and without music. The rhythm and step pattern will make sense and be much easier (trust me) if you follow the text, photos, and foot charts carefully. Once you feel comfortable with a foot pattern, put on the music and count it out for a moment. Almost any melody can be turned into a Waltz, Fox Trot, or whatever when the appropriate changes in beat and rhythm are applied.

Dances differ more in rhythm than they do in actual steps. Once the beat is in your head, move your feet to the music. You'll know you've got it right when your feet follow a pattern in time with the rhythm. Remember, the faster the music, the smaller your steps. Practice awhile. Then hold your partner and practice a few patterns together. Besides the steps, he'll also need to learn how to lead her, and she how to follow him. Both partners need to feel comfortable and at ease.

HE HAS HER IN THE PALM OF HIS HANDS

Traditional touch dancing impresses me as a sensual, chauvinistic game of follow the leader. He makes all the leadership decisions in advance (a fraction before each beat), and she's obliged to follow in his footsteps obediently.

He develops effective ways of giving meaningful

directional clues with his body: a twist of his shoulders, the way he leans his torso, a step in the right (or left) direction, the subtle pressure of his hands, all combine to make him a skillful leader. In closed position, for example, the gentle way he pushes or pulls his left hand, and the persuasive pressure of his right hand held firmly against her back, help her to respond more sensitively to his leadership.

With practice, partners eventually develop a responsive relationship. They become more relaxed, and she submits to his assuring lead by allowing him to manipulate her through a variety of different movements and positions!

STEPPING OUT IN STYLE

The kind of stepping you'll be doing in all the partner dances is remarkably similar. Every step pattern is based on a geometric shape: a square, a circle, or a line. You'll learn how to describe patterns using the appropriate rhythm for each dance. Then you'll be encouraged to combine different patterns or shapes in any way you like to make each dance come alive for you.

Unless indicated otherwise, every dance starts with feet together. His first step is forward on his left (L); her first step is backward on her right (R). Technically, each step starts from the hip, not the knee; the knees are relaxed. When stepping backward, slide your toes back first before letting the heel land with your weight on it.

In tea dancing (except for the Fox Trot), most forward steps start with the ball of the foot touching the floor before the heel, toes turned slightly out.

The personality you put into your dancing—the way you carry yourself, point your toes, feel the music—is called "style." Some dancers have an "old smoothie," relaxed, easygoing style; others prefer a more staccato, affected, exhibitionist flair. With practice you'll naturally begin to develop your own expressive response to the music and steps. When you move with style, your body responds with agility, grace, and coordination to the beat, as though you've been doing this sort of thing all your life.

There are a few stylistic no-no's that you should be aware of, lest you destroy the look and feel you're trying to develop. *Don't look at your feet.* This is the most difficult habit to break; it's so irresistible to drop your head and let your eyes do the dancing. You'll look like an ostrich.

Think tall and elegant. You can relax, but don't collapse. Keep your steps paced medium to small at first. Most beginners tend to take giant steps and wear themselves out trying to keep up with the music.

He signals directional changes with his body, not his mouth. (Please don't squeeze her hand too tightly while signaling, else gangrene could set in.)

From here, turn to the Glossary, and after you've made sense of it, flip to any dance of your choice, read the chapter introduction, then let loose!

It won't take long before you discover that there's something irresistible about touching someone close to you when you dance. This sort of commingling has been a consistently popular form of recreation for centuries, and from all indications, it is here to stay. So if you haven't already tried it, relax and let yourself enjoy a little intimacy in public dance places. Shall we dance?

GLOSSARY

CLOSED

PROMENADE (SEMI OPEN)

OPEN

TWO-HANDED BREAK

ONE-HANDED BREAK

FREE (FREE-STYLE)

HAND POSITIONS

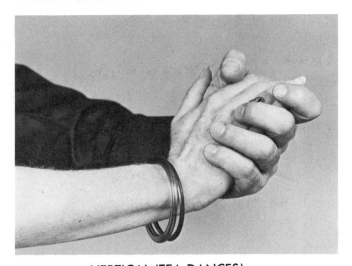

VERTICAL (TEA DANCES)

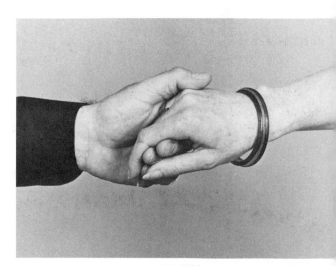

LINDY

PREPARING TO MAKE CONTACT **16**

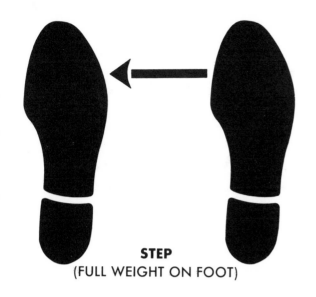

STEP
(FULL WEIGHT ON FOOT)

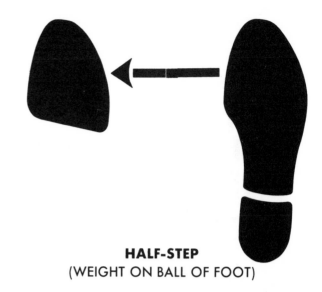

HALF-STEP
(WEIGHT ON BALL OF FOOT)

PIVOT
(PARTIAL TURN ON BALL OF FOOT)

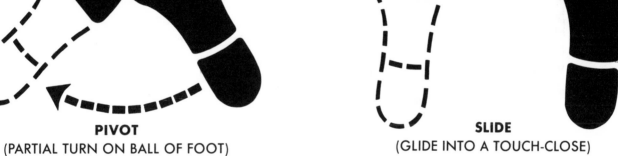

SLIDE
(GLIDE INTO A TOUCH-CLOSE)

LATIN

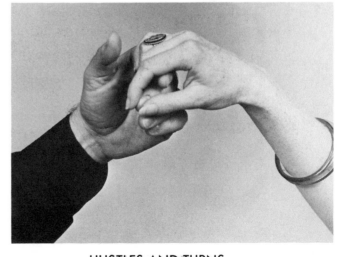

HUSTLES AND TURNS

CHAPTER TWO

CHIC TO CHIC: TEA DANCES

One of the first organizations to standardize ballroom dance steps as we know them today was the Imperial Society of Teachers and Dancers founded in England in 1924. European (especially English) dance teachers were eager to prescribe exact ways of dancing that could be judged right or wrong. Each dance was divided into three levels: bronze (beginner or social level), silver (intermediate), and gold (advanced, exhibition level). At every level, a dance had its own set of detailed rules and fastidious regulations based on English style. Judges could refer to a rule book to evaluate participants in ballroom competitions, and instructors used it to teach the International style.

The American style of ballroom dancing developed as a casual and practical answer to the formal International system. Americans simplified the steps and permitted individual expression, but retained the established conventions of male dominance and gallantry. The man always leads; technically, he "presents" the woman. Tea dances, except the Lindy, shared the same defined patterns, but they weren't danced with exactitude. The level system was retained, as was the counterclockwise line of direction around the dance floor to avoid collisions.

In this chapter and the next one, I've presented the most popular American-style bronze-level ballroom dances enjoyed today. I'll admit to adding a touch of silver for color, and I encourage you to add your own precious elements to make each dance shine for you.

Dance #1: Waltz on the Wild Side

When the Waltz was brought from Germany in the first half of the nineteenth century, it was considered a wild and shocking dance. The scandalous closeness of partners (better for balance, my dear) and the sheer speed of the couple's movement around the floor were assessed as lewd and lascivious! The Waltz was even banned in parts of Germany in the late eighteenth and early nineteenth centuries for being downright indecent and immoral! It wasn't until late in the nineteenth century that respectable Europeans dared to attempt the "closed" dance position. The French danced the Waltz with a formal, balletic, classical style. The Viennese preferred to speed around a ballroom until they were breathless.

Well, we've come a long way, baby. By the 1830s, Europe was witnessing "waltzing fever" and Johann Strauss was composing and playing the kind of waltzing music that set Viennese dancers on fire! The Waltz is the oldest tea or "social" dance that is still with us, and it's the only one in 3/4 time. As the German word indicates, waltzing is gliding smoothly around the floor. The style has a light, floating quality in the rise and fall of the body. The steps are long, wide strides, taken from the hip rather than the knee, to create a sweeping motion. So lighten up, Matilda, and think romantic!

Recommended Practice Music
Traditional: Johann Strauss
Standards: Al Goodman
Pop: *You Light up My Life* (Debby Boone)

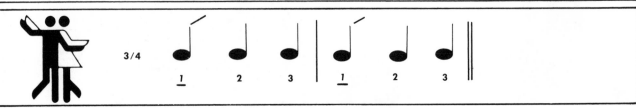

3/4

1　　2　　3　│　1　　2　　3

BASIC WALTZ STEP

The first beat is accented, so you'll be taking one healthy-sized step (forward or backward) with your foot flat on the floor, your knee bent, and your weight falling on the downbeat. On the second and third beats, your knees straighten and you rise onto the balls of your feet. In other words, you're lower on the first beat and higher on the next two beats.

You're describing an L shape on the floor. When this becomes comfortable, try traveling counterclockwise, then reverse direction, all in closed position.

BASIC WALTZ STEP

Counts	His	Hers
1	Step L forward	Step R backward
2	Step ball of R foot to side (half step)	Step ball of L foot to side (half step)
3	Step ball of L foot next to R	Step ball of R foot next to L
4	Step R forward	Step L backward
5	Step ball of L foot to side (half step)	Step ball of R foot to side (half step)
6	Close ball of R foot next to L	Close ball of L foot next to R

BOX STEP

If you dance the basic step forward and backward, and step diagonally sideways on the 2nd and 5th counts, you will have described a box or square pattern.

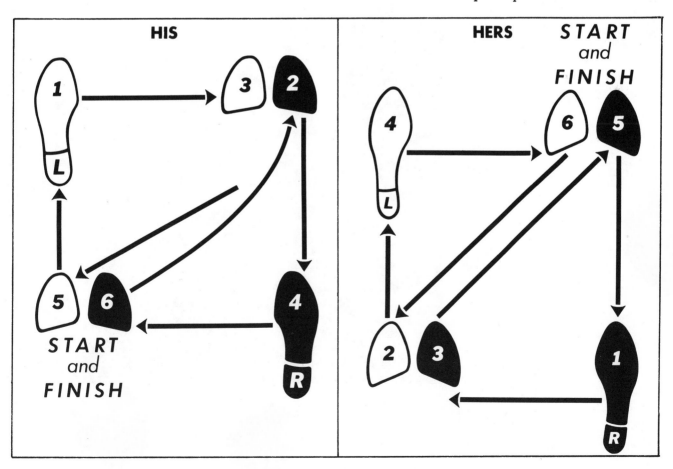

LEFT BOX TURN

You'll be doing four sets of the basic step, each ending with a quarter turn to the left. Follow in these footsteps, then once you've mastered the left turn, try the same turn to the right side with your partner in closed position.

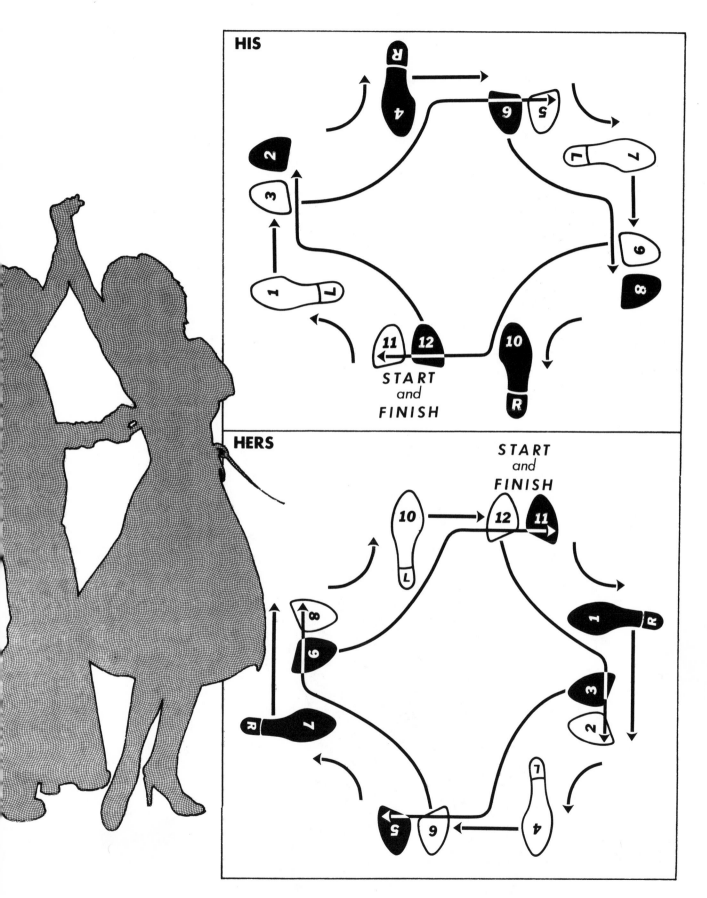

TWINKLE

Perhaps this is where that wonderful phrase "twinkle toes" originated. On the 2nd and 5th counts, he leads her on a diagonal over to his right, then left side.

Counts	His	Hers
1	Step L forward	Step R backward
2	Half-step R diagonally forward (toes turned in)	Half-step L diagonally backward (toes turned out)
3	Close L next to R (she's at your R side)	Close R next to L
4	Step R forward	Step L backward
5	Half-step L diagonally forward (toes turned in)	Half-step R diagonally backward (toes turned out)
6	Close R next to L (she's at your L side)	Close L next to R

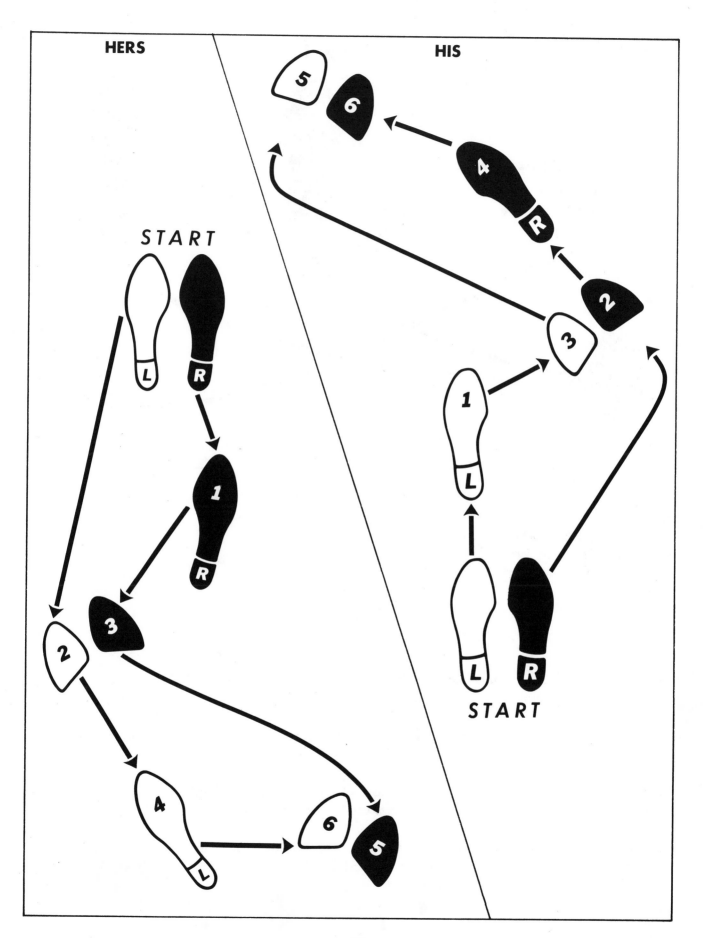

START

START

TEA DANCES

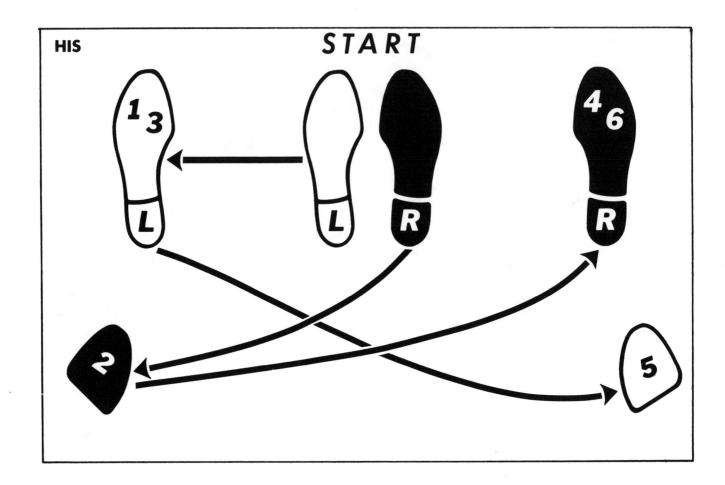

BALANCE STEPS

*There are at least four ways to
do a balance step: forward,
backward, sideways, and
side crossing.*

COUNTS:	1	2	3	4
Forward:	Step 1 foot forward	Half-step other foot next to it	Step 1st foot in place	Reverse feet
Backward:	Step 1 foot backward	Half-step other foot next to it	Step 1st foot in place	Reverse feet
Sideways:	Step 1 foot to side	Half-step other foot next to it	Step 1st foot in place	Reverse feet
Cross: (Cross balance)	Step 1 foot to side	Half-step other foot behind 1st foot	Step 1st foot in place	Reverse feet and direction

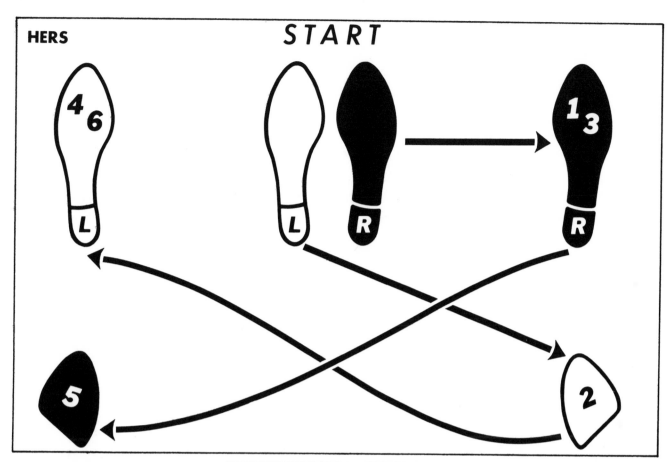

The balance steps combine well with any other Waltz steps. Try a balance followed by a basic, or a balance with a partial left box turn (three counts).

A WILDER WALTZ:

What makes waltzing wild is the speed with which you combine basics and variations, adding a dash of fancy footwork occasionally for your own individual stamp (so to speak). As long as you stick to the basics (the first step long and low, the second step high, and the third "closed"), you can introduce any wild concoction you like. Start with the variations given here so that you get a feel for the rhythm and steps. Combine them in any order. Dance as many of one variation as you like before changing to another. Then try innovating steps, turns, pivots, and positions with your partner. Don't be afraid to try a new variation, as long as it keeps you on your toes! Now let yourself glide through the air with the greatest of ease!

Here's a wild combination to give you some ideas.

4 Waltz basics

2 balance steps (forward/backward)

2 balance steps (side to side)

4 twinkles

2 hesitations

1 left box turn

4 travel half turns

4 balance steps (cross)

1 box step

2 underarm turns

2 your own creation

DANCE #2: THE FOXY TROT

Stories about the origins of this dance center around the name Harry Fox. Some identify him as a Ziegfeld Follies performer who, in a 1914 performance, introduced a kind of jerky, trotting sequence of steps to ragtime music. The public, captivated by his movements, began to perform them in popular ballrooms. Supposedly the original twelve energetic steps were drastically modified, slowed, and smoothed out over the next few years to the three-step and four-step versions we know today.

Other stories refer to Harry Fox as a bandleader in 1914 in New York, who modified ragtime music. The dancers responded by combining the One-Step and Two-Step and calling the mixture the Fox Trot.

Whatever the exact origin, the medium-to-slow version of the Fox Trot is still the perennial standby of ballroom dances. What we now call "slow dancing" is really the Fox Trot, a dance so simple that you, too, will be hot to trot!

For easier learning, I'll break this dance down into four rhythm patterns. The two most common are the "one-slow-step" (not to be confused with the dance the "One-Step") and the "two-slow-step" patterns. After you practice the basics, throw in a dash of style and a few variations. Then combine these with the next two patterns and you'll be innovating in your own foxy way.

Recommended Practice Music:
Traditional: Scott Joplin
Standards: Guy Lombardo, Tommy Dorsey

PATTERN A: THE ONE-SLOW-STEP BASIC

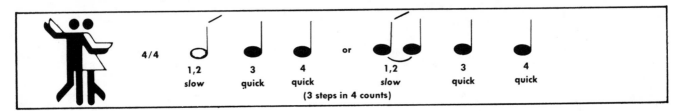

4/4   1,2 slow   3 quick   4 quick   or   1,2 slow   3 quick   4 quick

(3 steps in 4 counts)

This is the easiest of the four patterns, so let's start here.

	His	**Hers**
1 ⎫	Step L forward	Step R backward ⎫
2 ⎭	Hold	Hold
3	Step R diagonally forward (in line with L)	Step L diagonally backward (in line with R)
4	Step L next to R	Step R next to L

(step is completed when heel lowers to the floor)

5 ⎫	Step R forward	Step L backward
6 ⎭	Hold	Hold
7	Step L diagonally forward	Step R diagonally forward
8	Step R next to L	Step L next to R

Notice that your feet are describing an L and that you start and end with your feet together. Continue traveling in the same direction until the steps feel comfortable, then practice the same pattern in the reverse direction. Loosen up your knees, and give them a bit of bounce with each medium-sized step you take, so you're sprightly stepping through the madding crowd.

Once you become adept at this, try traveling in closed position in a circle counterclockwise around the room. Even though you may never dance in a formal ballroom, you may want to familiarize yourself with the traditional "line" (really circle) of direction.

Step is complete when heel touches the floor.

TROT BOX STEP

If the floor becomes too crowded to really trot around, try this box step.

		His	Hers
1		Step L forward	Step R backward
2		Hold	Hold
3		Step R diagonally forward and level with L	Step L diagonally backward and level with R
4		Step L next to R	Step R next to L
5		Step R backward	Step L forward
6		Hold	Hold
7		Step L diagonally backward, even with R	Step R diagonally forward, even with L
8		Close R next to L	Close L next to R

Practice the box step a few times, then pass go and pick up the box turn.

33

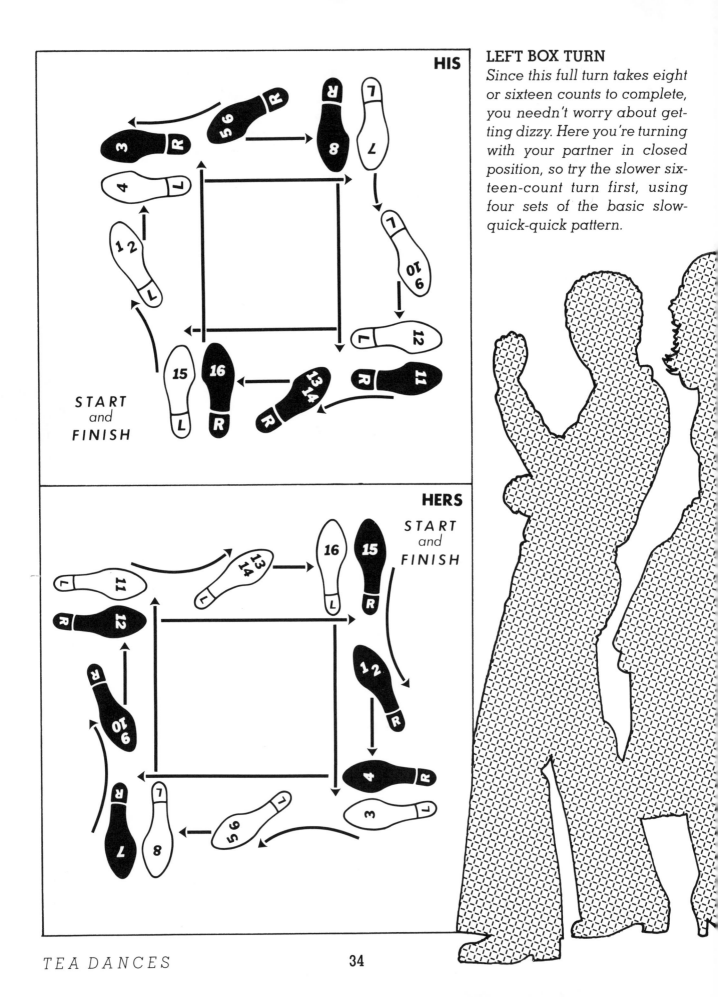

HIS

START
and
FINISH

HERS

START
and
FINISH

LEFT BOX TURN

Since this full turn takes eight or sixteen counts to complete, you needn't worry about getting dizzy. Here you're turning with your partner in closed position, so try the slower sixteen-count turn first, using four sets of the basic slow-quick-quick pattern.

Counts	His	Hers
1	Step L forward, turning toes out slightly	Step R backward (toes turned slightly inward)
2	Hold	Hold
3	Step R forward and ¼ turned to L	Step L backward and ¼ turned to R
4	Close L next to R	Close R next to L
5	*Step R backward (toes turned slightly inward)*	Step L forward (toes slightly outward)
6	*Hold*	Hold
7	Step L diagonally backward	Step R diagonally forward
8	Close R next to L	Close L next to R

You're halfway around now, and to finish this box turn, all you do is repeat counts 1–8 from where you are now. Try the turn again, this time to the right side. (If you can do it to one side, you can do it to the other!) From here, see if you can complete the turn in eight counts (left and right side).

OPEN TWINKLE

As in the Waltz, a "twinkle"
rounds out the corners of an
L-shaped or stairstep pattern.
You'll be starting in closed
position, opening to prome-
nade, then ending closed.

Use this twinkle anytime you
want to cut corners on the
dance floor.

	His	*Hers*
1	Step L forward	Step R backward
2	Hold	Hold
3	Step R forward (turn toes in) and open to promenade position	Step L backward (turn toes in) and open to promenade position
4	Step L next to R	Step R next to L
5	Cross R over L (step R forward)	Cross L over R (step L forward)
6	Hold	Hold
7	Step L sideways (toes turned in) and return to closed position	Step R sideways (toes turned in) and return to closed position
8	Close R to L	Close L to R

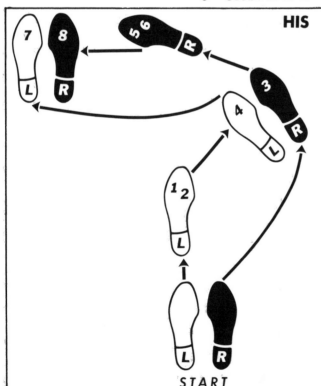

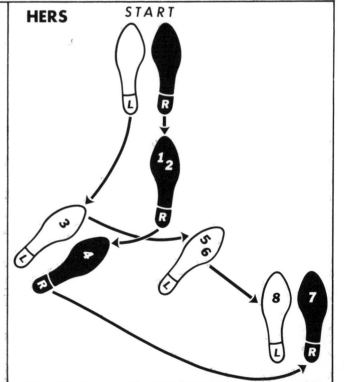

SIDE TROT

Here's another handy step to use when the floor is crowded or when you're pondering your next move.

Counts	His	Hers
1	Step L sideways	Step R sideways
2	Hold	Hold
3	Step R sideways	Step L sideways
4	Close L next to R	Close R next to L
5–8	Repeat counts 1–4, starting with the opposite foot	

The above steps should keep you busy for a while. Combine them as you like, then move on to pattern B.

TEA DANCES

PATTERN B: TWO-SLOW-STEP BASIC

As you can discern, you're merely adding another slow step (two counts) to pattern A. Every variation in the previous pages can also be accomplished using this pattern; all you do is add another slow step.

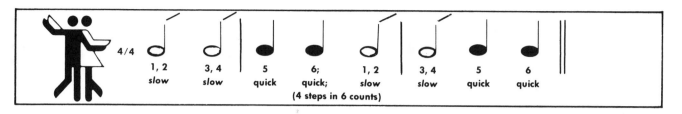

Counts	His	Hers
1	Step L forward	Step R backward
2	Hold	Hold
3	Step R forward	Step L backward
4	Hold	Hold
5	Step L sideways	Step R sideways
6	Close R next to L	Close L next to R

Close is completed when heel is lowered and weight is on full foot

| 7–12 | (Repeat counts 1–6) | |

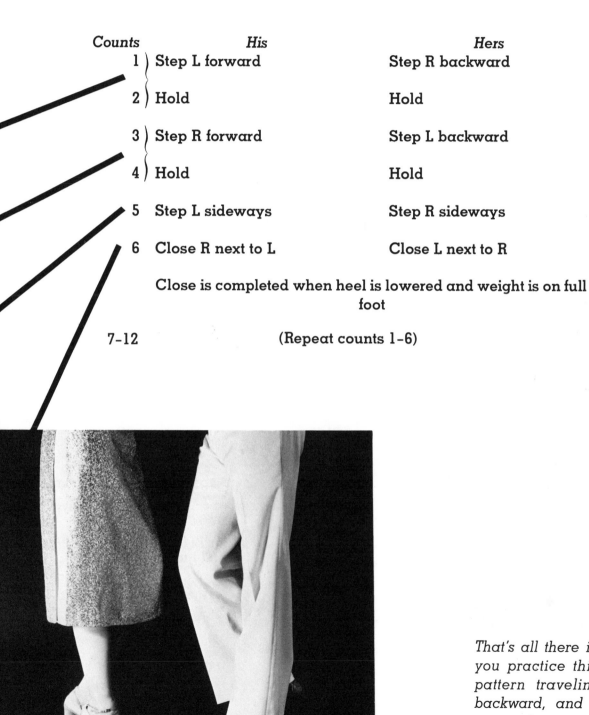

That's all there is to it! After you practice this L-shaped pattern traveling forward, backward, and around the room (counterclockwise), you'll be ready for a few variations.

TEA DANCES

OPEN WALK

Here you're dropping your clasped hands and walking side by side during the two slow steps. For the two quick steps, you may return to closed position or remain side by side. It is your choice.

HALF TURNS

Here you're taking two slow steps in one direction, making a half turn on the two quick steps, then taking two slow steps again in the reverse, a half turn on the quickies, etc., back and forth. This is actually much easier that you'd imagine. Try it.

VARIATION: SPIN TURNS

Every once in a while he might like to spin her under his left arm a few times as a change of pace from all that trotting.

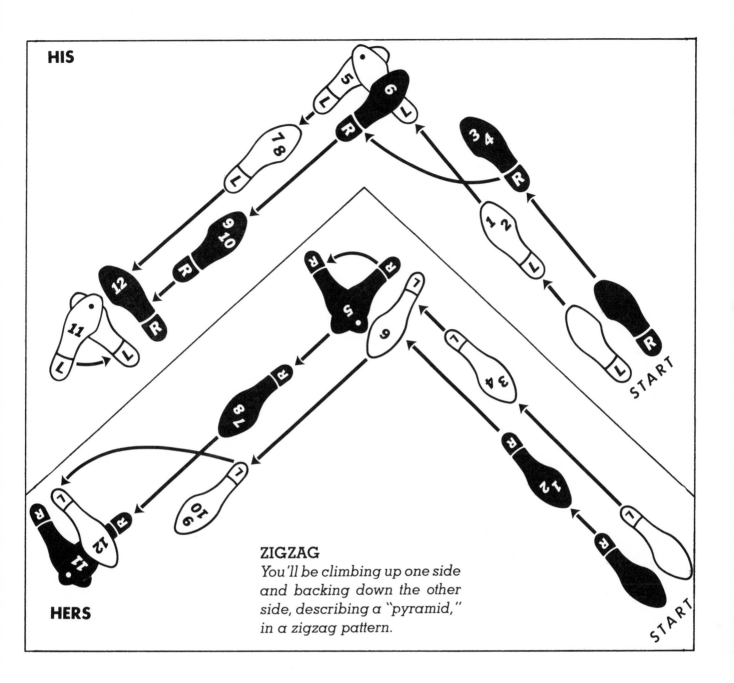

HIS

HERS

ZIGZAG
You'll be climbing up one side and backing down the other side, describing a "pyramid," in a zigzag pattern.

Before we move on to the other two patterns in the Fox Trot, why not take a moment to see if you can combine a few of the basic steps from patterns A and B, then mix up the two rhythms for variety? If this still feels elementary, the following patterns should keep you hopping!

PATTERN C: THREE SLOW STEPS

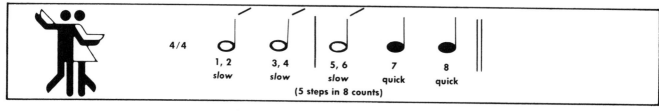

4/4 — 1, 2 slow — 3, 4 slow — 5, 6 slow — 7 quick — 8 quick
(5 steps in 8 counts)

Start forward or backward, then apply this pattern to the previous step variations. Don't panic!

PATTERN D: FOUR QUICK STEPS

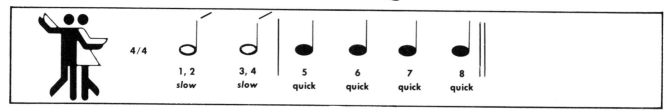

4/4 — 1, 2 slow — 3, 4 slow — 5 quick — 6 quick — 7 quick — 8 quick

MAKING IT FOXY

It's what you do with what you know that makes you a fox on the dance floor. Practice until you've got your slows and quicks together, then add a few variations without missing a beat. Now transcend the prescribed and innovate a few variations of your own. Just remember to begin your variations with feet together, make at least your first step a slow one, and end your variation with at least two quick steps that bring the feet together. In other words, start slowly, end quickly, and stay together. Think loose knees. Good luck, You're on!

DANCE #3: THE TEMPESTUOUS TANGO

When the Tango was introduced from Buenos Aires at the end of the nineteenth century, it was considered exotic and suggestive. It didn't become a rage until it was modified and standardized so that it could be "respectably" danced in the casino ballrooms of the early 1900s. By 1915, "Tango Clubs" had proliferated. Restaurants with dance floors (yes, indeed, it's been done before!) had small Argentinian Tango orchestras providing live accompaniment for the tea dancers in the "clubs." The original Tango underwent numerous changes over the years, and was finally standardized in its present form in the twenties.

Of all ballroom dances, this one is probably the most stylized and dramatic. There's no bouncing around in the Tango; the steps are long, smooth, and sleek, with the feet kept close to the floor. Each dance phrase is punctuated by a pregnant, poised pause, and begins with a quick head jerk that adds to the dramatic style. You can't carry off the Tango with stooped posture, so straighten up, lift your head high, point your nose into the future, and think sleek.

The Tango can be danced in either 2/4 or 4/4 time, but it will be easier to learn in 4/4.

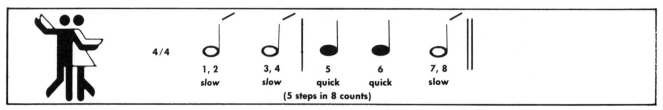

4/4

1, 2	3, 4	5	6	7, 8
slow	slow	quick	quick	slow

(5 steps in 8 counts)

Recommended Practice Music:
Standards: *Hernando's Hideaway* (any version), *Tango!* (Mantovani)

Like the Foxy Trot, the rhythm patterns of slows and quicks in the Tango may be varied, as long as the dance phrase ends on the eighth count. First learn the basic two slow steps. Here goes.

TANGO BASIC

Counts	*His*	*Hers*
1	Long step L forward	Long step R backward
2	Hold	Hold
3	Long step R forward	Long step L backward
4	Hold	Hold
5	Short step L forward	Short step R backward
6	Short step R diagonally forward (level with L)	Short step L diagonally backward (level with R)
7	Slide and touch	Slide and touch
8	L next to R	R next to L

Practice this basic forward and backward until it feels fairly natural, then move along to other variations.

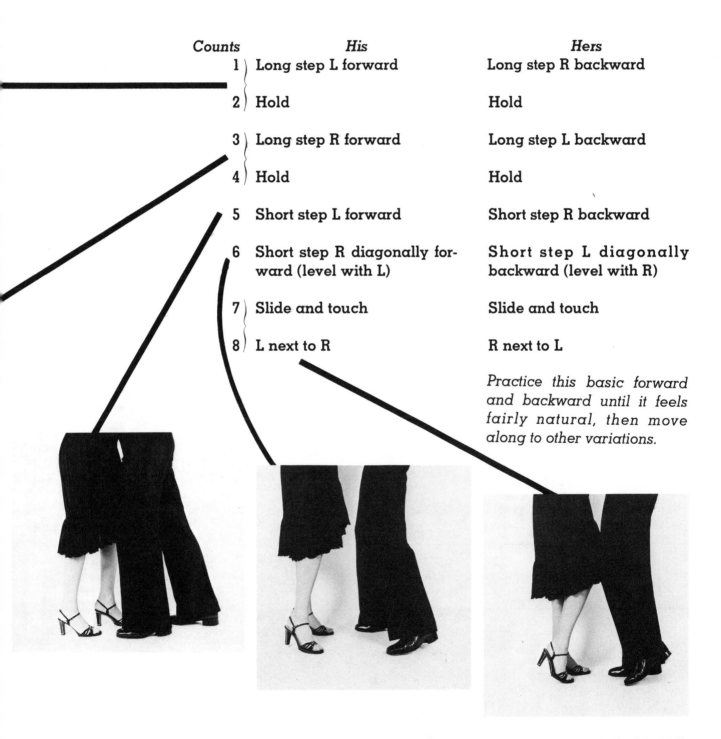

FOOT CHARTS OVERLEAF

45

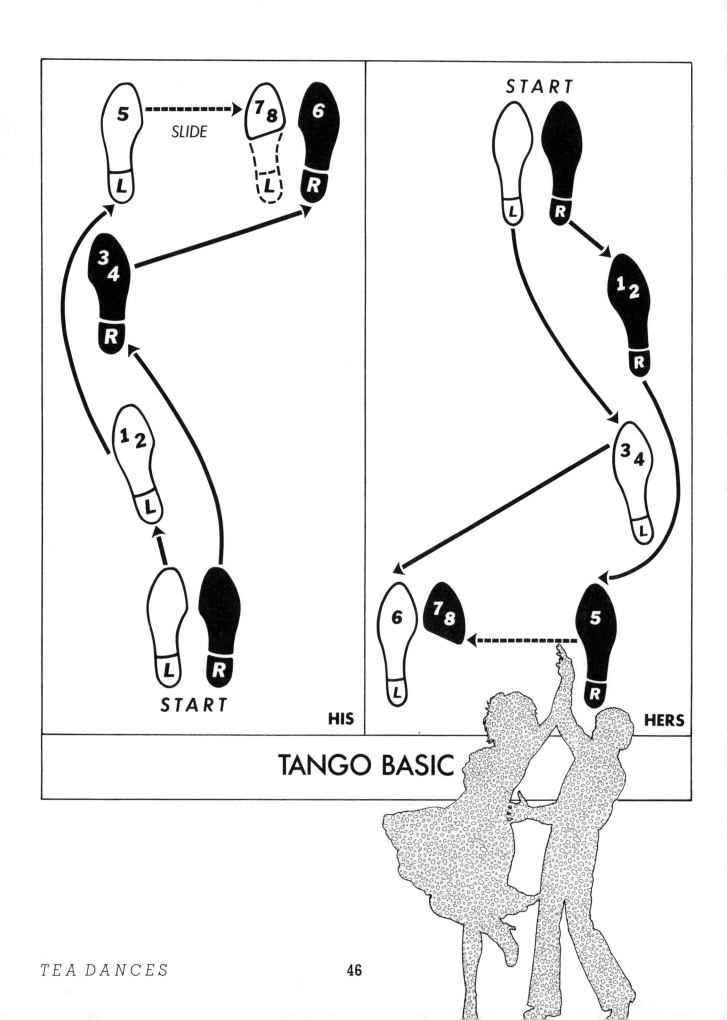

TANGO BASIC

HIS

5 L — SLIDE → 7 8 L   6 R

3 4 R

1 2 L

START L R

HERS

START L R

1 2 R

3 4 L

6 L   7 8   5 R

TANGO DIP (CORTÉ)

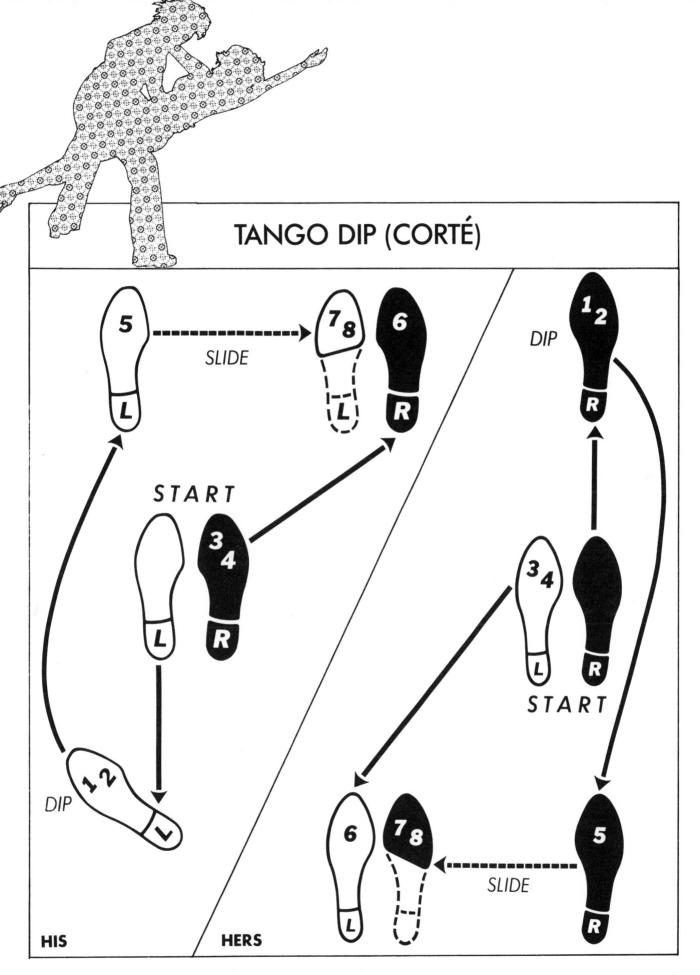

SLIDE

START

DIP

HIS

DIP

START

SLIDE

HERS

TEA DANCES

TANGO DIP (CORTÉ)

This variation is really more of a lean than a dip, but if you throw yourself into it, you'll find it quite tempestuous. The Corté may be substituted for any two slow steps (four counts) of any Tango variation. Here it is combined with the basic step. Stay close to your partner (but don't become too entangled).

	His	Hers
1	Long step L forward and lean over (L knee bent, R straight)	Long step R backward and lean backward (R knee bent, L straight)
2	Hold	Hold
3	Rock backward on R (L stays in place)	Rock forward on L
4	Hold	Hold
5	Short step L forward	Short step R backward
6	Short step R to side	Short step L to side
7	Slide and touch L	Slide and touch R
8	next to R	next to L

CORTÉ Turn

After you've "dipped" yourself dizzy, try this related variation. On counts 5–8, turn with your partner in closed position just by taking little steps together in a circle (a step for every count). Try this variation a few times in succession, then combine with the basic step. Now you're ready to move right along to the Tango Promenade.

TANGO PROMENADE

In this case, he'll be stepping sideways while she pivots in the same direction.

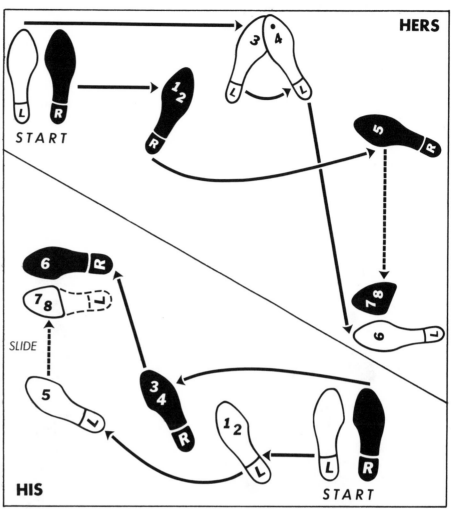

Counts	*His*	*Hers*
1	Step L sideways and turn into open position	Step R sideways and turn into open position
2	Hold	Hold
3	Step-cross R forward	Cross-pivot L (¼ turn L)
4	Hold	Hold
5	Step L forward into closed position (turned ¼)	Step R backward into closed position
6	Step R to side	Step L to side
7	Slide-touch L	Slide-touch
8	next to R	R to L

Repeat counts 1–8

TEMPESTUOUS CRISSCROSS

Here's a quick change of pace. You'll both be turned around a bit in the second step.

Counts	His	Hers
1	Step L to side and twist L a bit	Step R to side and twist R a bit
2	Hold	Hold
3	Cross R in front of L	Cross L in front of R
4	Pivot on R and about-face	Pivot on L and about-face

5	Cross L over R	Cross R over L
6	Step R to side	Step L to side
7	Slide-touch	Slide-touch
8	L next to R	R next to L

You may repeat this, then combine with other patterns.

TANGO RUNNING STEPS

These will keep you a bit more active. You can "run" forward, backward, sideways, or turning in closed position. Try two slow walking steps first (counts 1–4, he starts with the left and she with the right), then "run" on counts 5–8 (four quick steps). If you're turning together, her right foot will need to be almost between his feet on the running steps. Notice that the rhythm changes.

TEMPESTUOUS TOUCHES

To carry off the Tango with style, you and your partner will need to synchronize your footwork. Hold every slow step until the very end of the count (don't cheat the beat) before stepping again. Try to end each dance phrase with a clean, sharp stop (just as the musical phrases end) and start with a sharp head twist in the direction in which you're heading. Feel free to combine the steps and patterns to your own liking.

Try a Corté with running steps, or a crisscross after a basic. Then be inventive and ad lib a turn or two to the various Tango rhythms. Keep your upper body close to your partner's and glide smoothly together step by step into the sunset. Remember it takes two to tangle.

Add your own tempestuous touches to this combination:

2 basics

2 crisscrosses

1 basic

1 Corté with 4 running steps

1 Corté

1 crisscross

1 promenade turn

2 your own thing

DANCE #4: THE LUSTY LINDY (LINDY HOP, SWING, JITTERBUG)

When Charles Lindbergh flew solo over the Atlantic in 1927, people commemorated the event by naming all sorts of things after him, including a wild novelty dance popular at the time that was christened the "Lindy Hop." In the thirties, the steps were revised slightly to synchronize with Swing music played by big bands of twenty-five to forty highly trained musicians. By the late nineteen thirties the Lindy became known as the "Swing," and everyone was struck with Swing fever. Across the country each neighborhood had its own style of swinging. Teens in particular went Swing crazy (you thought only disco made teens feverish?), and some wilder spinoffs (pardon the pun), such as the Crazy Shag and the Jitterbug, began to develop. The latter is reported to have come out of Harlem in the thirties, and embraces a wilder, more exhibitionlike style with some improvised steps. The "closed" and "break" positions with aerial lifts and jumps (real athletic feats) and the furious footwork made the dancers resemble a bunch of "jittery bugs"; hence the name.

Today, the Lindy or Swing is a ballroom dance whose popularity has endured. With a slight modification, the Lindy-Swing of the 1920s and 1930s has become the Latin-Swing Hustle of the 1970s (and you thought there was something new under the sun?).

Unlike such tea dances as the Waltz, Fox Trot, and Tango, which travel counterclockwise around the room, the Lindy is a "spot" dance done in a small area that dancers carve out around themselves on the floor. Also, the Lindy is done mostly in the break position rather than in the closed "social dance" position. Since you and your partner spend time dancing apart in the break position, the Lindy allows freedom for individual nuance and interpretation. You'll want to practice your style until it's very loose, bouncy, and sprightly, 'cause "it don't mean a thing if it ain't got that swing!"

THE DOUBLE LINDY

Swing music is written in 2/4 and 4/4 time, but for simplicity's sake we'll learn the steps in 2/4.

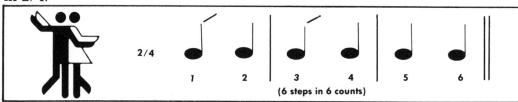

2/4   1   2   3   4   5   6

(6 steps in 6 counts)

The two popular versions of this dance are the Double Lindy (six steps) and the Triple Lindy (eight steps). With both versions, you begin in a promenade position for the first few bars of music, then the rest of the time you're dancing and turning mostly in break position (holding one or both hands with your partner). Try the double step first.

Basic Double Lindy

There are a few different versions of this step; here's one of the more popular. Try it alone, then in break position with your partner.

Counts	His	Hers
1	Tap L to side (slightly)	Tap R to side (slightly)
2	Step L in place (where tapped)	Step R in place (where tapped)
3	Tap R to side	Tap L to side
4	Step R where tapped	Step L where tapped
5	Step L backward (twist L)	Step R backward (twist to R)
6	Step R in place (face forward)	Step L in place (face forward)

Most of the time you'll be dancing in the break position. Face your partner and hold hands. Now dance holding hands for the first four counts (tap, step; tap, step). On the fifth count, he gently pushes her back with either his left or right hand and releases that hand at the same time, causing her to step backward a bit farther (while he steps backward on his left foot). There should be a pulling tension. Since you each have a free arm on this count, instead of dangling it, raise it skyward. On the sixth count, face each other again and hold both hands.

Pull apart from each other on the fifth count with a bit more tension (and for better balance), then come a little closer on counts 1 and 2.

TEA DANCES

ROCK BASIC
(PROMENADE)

Usually the Lindy or Swing begins in this promenade position, where partners remain for only a brief few bars. Then the man throws or turns her out (please don't take this too literally) and partners find themselves in break position.

His and Hers

1 Tap front foot and lean forward

2 Step on front foot

3 Tap back foot

4 Step on back foot

5 Step front foot diagonally backward and twist apart slightly

6 Step opposite foot in place and face forward again

Repeat this "rock" forward and backward a few more times before he turns her into a one-handed break position. An underarm turn on counts 5 and 6 will put you in break position.

BASIC TRIPLE LINDY
(EAST COAST SWING)

Here you're adding an extra "and" count, so the footwork becomes a triplet of steps on each side, and a bit of light tripping for your fast feet.

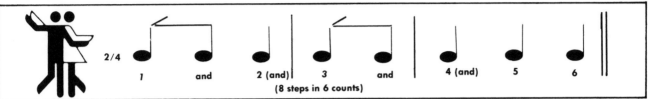

Counts	His	Hers
1	Step L to side	Step R to side
and	Quick slide R to L	Quick slide L to R
2	Repeat count 1	Repeat count 1
3	Step R to side	Step L to side
and	Quick slide L to R	Quick slide R to L
4	Step R to side	Step L to side
5	Half-step L to back (slightly back-crossed)	Half-step R to back (slightly back-crossed)
6	Step R in place	Step L in place

If you have any knowledge of tap dancing, you may also think of the pattern as: step-ball-change (sideways); step-ball-change (other side); back, step. (Hope this helps.) Practice this version until your feet can move with some semblance of speed, then put on a record, and swing.

Lusty Hints
Whether you do the Double or Triple Lindy (or mix up the two), he starts left and she starts right and your feet travel sideways. You'll be closer together on the first two steps, and you'll break apart on the last two steps. In other words, start close, break off, then spin around in a daze. Yes, turns are the most creative aspect of this dance. "Turn" to Chapter Four and try to incorporate some of the turns described there into your Lindy. To start a turn from the rock basic (promenade) position, he pushes her waist and lifts his left arm simultaneously to gently coax her under. While you're turning, don't ignore your feet. Whatever turn you select or innovate, it is your footwork that maintains the constant Lindy rhythm. It's a challenge to coordinate your feet with positions and turns, so smile at your partner occasionally for encouragement and keep the bounce in your knees and feet, where they belong. People who swing together, stay together.

TEA DANCES

CHAPTER THREE

SPICY SALSA: HOT LATIN

"Salsa" is the Spanish word for hot sauce: a mixture of spices simmering in a savory Spanish stew. Delicious taste. Recently the word has come to mean "hot Latin music": a mixture of Afro-Cuban jazz simmering in savory Spanish sounds. Delicious music. Salsa music has its roots in the rhythms of African slaves brought to Cuba in the nineteenth century. The ingredients of hot Afro rhythms and earthy Indian-Spanish gypsy music were stirred into a tasty musical treat.

It wasn't until the 1940s, when Havana became the "in" resort spot for Americans, that Cuban music was discovered and exported to this country. The Afro-Cuban rhythms mixed well with American big-band sounds of the forties, and the fusion produced some popular dance music throughout the forties and fifties. In the fifties and early sixties, "Latin Jazz" was confined mostly to the barrios of Miami, New York, and Los Angeles. It wasn't until the mid-sixties that several leading Latin musicians and composers decided to band together and popularize "Salsa," as they called it. Salsa music incorporates layers of strings, brass, reeds, and drums to create a driving dance beat with counterbeats and thick, rich rhythms. Vocals are often added for additional flavor. The result is several spicy rhythms all bubbling at once. When you get a whiff of a riff, your feet want to burn up the dance floor!

DANCES

When the word "Salsa" is used in a general sense, it refers to the type of Latin music and dancing, just as "Disco" refers to both the music and style of dancing. There's no dance called "the Disco"; likewise there's no such dance as "the Salsa."

Salsa's basic dance is the Mambo. In addition to the dances presented in this chapter, other Cuban dance variations are frequently performed to salsa music: the Bolero (slow Rumba in closed position), the Guaracha (fast Rumba), the Cumbia (a side-stepping Mambo), the Plena, Pachanga, Guaguanco, Mozambique, and High Life, to name a few.

All Latin dances are done in a small area (they don't travel around the room), and the footwork is kept small while the hips sway and the shoulders shimmy with sensuous control. A wonderful variety of positions awaits the Latin dancer: closed, open, break, and free-style. In free-style position, your arms are bent waist high and they roll around as if you were playing maracas right along with the band. The way you blend positions and turns depends on your individual taste. So set down your cool Cuba Libra and let the spicy Salsa sounds sweep you off your feet!

DANCE #5: THE RACY RUMBA

Rumba roots go back over four hundred years to the religious and ceremonial dances of African slaves transported to Cuba. Originally, the dance was a pantomime that evolved from an exhibitionist expression into a variety of different steps. When the Afro-Cuban Rumba was transported to Europe and the United States in the 1920s, it was exotic, erotic, and seductive, what with all that hip and shoulder shaking going on. By the 1940s, the ever-sedate English ballroom dance instructors had modified, diluted, and standardized the dance into a box pattern (rather than a traveling pattern around the room). The modified Rumba was immediately adopted by ballroom dancers everywhere.

It does seem that much of the raw soul of the ancestral dances has been lost through the process of homogenization over the years. However, when combined with the newer Salsa sounds, the Rumba can reclaim some of the abandon of its original style.

Recommended Practice Music:
Standards: Xavier Cugat, Noro Morales
Salsa: Congas Y Comparsas
Pop/Disco: *How Deep Is Your Love* (Bee Gees)

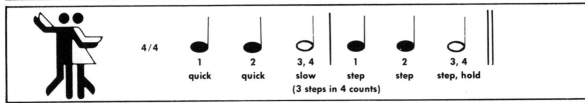

4/4

| 1 | 2 | 3, 4 | 1 | 2 | 3, 4 |
| quick | quick | slow | step | step | step, hold |

(3 steps in 4 counts)

Rumba music is composed in 2/4 or 4/4 time and it can be played in slow, medium, or fast tempo.

EL CUADRO (BASIC BOX STEP)

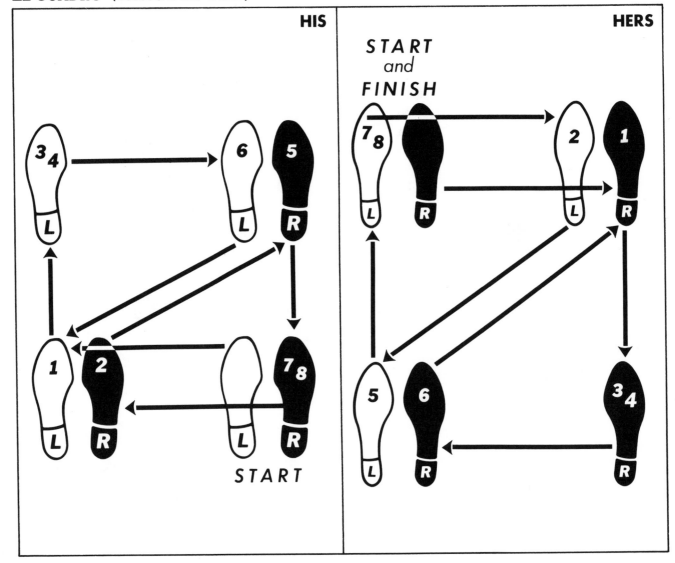

EL CUADRO (BASIC BOX STEP)

Counts	His	Hers
1	Step L to side	Step R to side
2	Close R to L	Close L to R
3	Step L forward	Step R forward
4	Hold	Hold
5	Step R diagonally forward, level with L	Step L diagonally forward, level with R
6	Close L to R	Close R to L
7	Step R backward	Step L backward
8	Hold	Hold

This is the basic Rumba pattern. Once you master it, try the left box turn in closed position.

RUMBA STYLE (OR "CUBAN MOTION")

Absolutely essential to the Rumba is the Cuban hip motion that gives this dance its style. If your hips aren't waving from side to side like palm leaves in the breeze, then you're not doing the Rumba. Let's analyze this characteristic hip sway.

Step on your left foot and throw your left hip to the side. Do the same to the right. Whichever foot you step on, swing that hip out on the same side. The step is taken on a flat foot, but the knees are kept relaxed. Imagine that you're impatiently waiting in line, shifting your weight from side to side (hip out when you shift), and you've got the idea. Now shift smoothly as you take very small steps with knees slightly bent. Once you've made a hip breakthrough by shifting in place, try to keep the sway while stepping sideways, forward, and backward. In no time, your hips should be as fluid as tequila. In learning the following dance patterns, take small steps, and try to concentrate most of your body movement into your hips.

LEFT BOX TURN

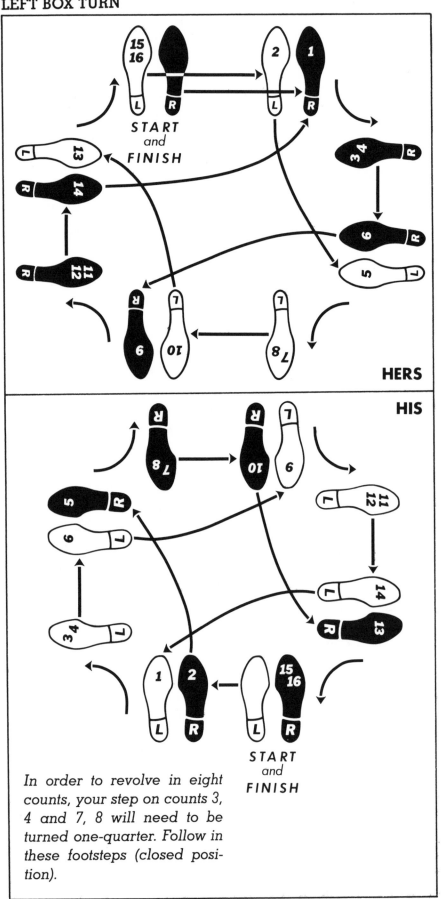

HERS

HIS

In order to revolve in eight counts, your step on counts 3, 4 and 7, 8 will need to be turned one-quarter. Follow in these footsteps (closed position).

RUMBA BUTTERFLY BREAK

This is a graceful, back-crossing break (not a back-breaking cross) that can get you from closed to open position. Start in closed position.

	His	*Hers*
1	Cross L behind R, release L hand (turn into open position)	Cross R behind L (turn into open position)
2	Step R in place	Step L in place
3	Step L into closed position	Step R into closed position
4	Hold	Hold
5	Step R behind L, release R hand, and turn out (open position)	Step L behind R, and turn out to open position
6	Step L in place	Step R in place
7	Step R into closed position	Step L into closed position
8	Hold	Hold

Repeat as often as you like. You don't have to butterfly to both sides. If you like, you can do the butterfly to only one side (counts 1–4 or counts 5–8) for a few times, then fly on to another variation, sort of half-winging it. The same goes for the crossover.

65   *HOT LATIN DANCES*

CUBAN ROCK

Here's a variation of the basic box step in which you're still in closed position, rocking back and forth on counts 6, 7 and 10, 11. "Rock" means changing weight or leaning back and forth without taking steps.

Counts	His	Hers
1	Step L to side	Step R to side
2	Close R to L	Close L to R
3	Step L forward	Step R backward
4	Hold	Hold
5	Step R forward	Step L backward
6	Rock back on L (weight on L)	Rock forward on R (weight on R)
7	Rock forward on R	Rock backward on L
8	Hold	Hold
9	Step L forward	Step R backward
10	Rock back on R	Rock forward on L
11	Rock forward on L	Rock back on R
12	Hold	Hold
13	Step R to side	Step L to side
14	Close L to R	Close R to L
15	Step R backward	Step L forward
16	Hold	Hold

This rock pattern is really a lot easier than it looks!

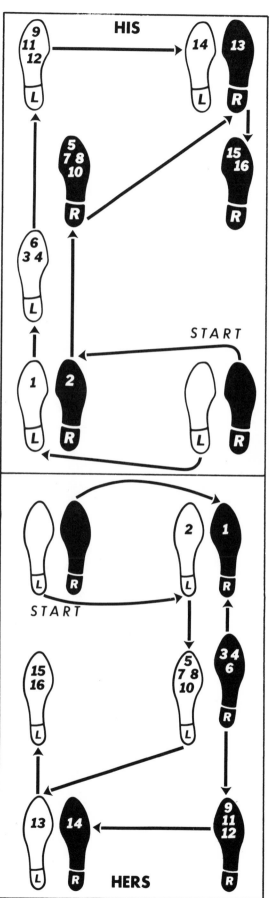

HOT LATIN DANCES

RUMBA CROSSOVER BREAK

You'll be crossing forward and turning sideways. Start in closed position.

	His	*Hers*
1	Pivot on R (to R) and simultaneously cross-step L over R (release R hand)	Pivot on L (to L) and cross-step R over L (break L hand)
2	Step R to side	Step L to side
3	Close L to R	Close R to L
4	Hold	Hold
5	Still holding her same hand, pivot on L to L and cross-step R over L	Pivot on R to R and cross-step L over R
6	Step L to side	Step R to side
7	Close R to L	Close L to R
8	Hold	Hold

OPEN CUBAN WALK

You're in a one-handed break position and you're simply "walking" circles around each other, keeping the Rumba rhythm and hip sways. Try to complete one full circle in eight counts. It is customary for his left hand to hold her right hand while he describes a circle by stepping backward and she Rumbas forward in a circle pattern. Every (little) step counts to help you draw circles around each other. One way to begin the Open Cuban Walk is by dancing a basic box step first. Then he releases his right hand from her left, and leads her into a circle with his left hand. You might try alternating boxes with circles for a while!

HOT LATIN DANCES

WHEEL TURN (OPEN SPOT TURN)

This one can be danced in either open or closed position, either forward or backward, with one foot serving as the central axis around which you circle. For break position, stand side by side, facing the opposite direction from your partner, and join inside hands (elbows bent). Now dance the Rumba steps, keeping your inside foot in the middle and describing the circle with your outside foot.

Change direction without skipping a beat!

RUMBA DOS-A-DO

Yes, it's the same variation as the one used in American Square Dancing, only in the Rumba, you're doing the Cuban Walk. Face your partner, "walk" forward (pass right shoulders), pass back to back, "walk" backward (pass left shoulders), and return "home." Remember to keep those hips swaying horizontally and your steps small.

DANCE #6: THE SENSUOUS SAMBA (BOSSA NOVA)

Although the Samba is usually classified as a Latin-American dance, it originated with African slaves transported to Brazil when it was first colonized.

SENSUOUS STYLING

The excitement created in this dance comes not from the steps (which are very simple), but from the style. The Samba is characterized by a teetering from side to side, or a rocking back and forth, as if you were bobbing up-down, forward-backward, like a rubber duck in a bathtub. To attain this Samba style, you'll need springy knees. Bend the knees on the first step, straighten them on the second, bend them again on the third. Each step is taken with a flat foot. This will make more sense when you try it in Samba rhythm. After you can bend-straighten-bend to rhythm, you'll need to learn how to make those moves sensuous.

Practice, rocking your pelvis forward and backward. Whenever you step forward, push your pelvis forward (knees bent a bit); when stepping backward, stick out your bottom (hips backward and knees bent, giving a "rolling" look to your body). Well, don't just sit there trying to figure this out. Stand up and start counting!

Lent season has always been celebrated in Brazil with a series of carnivals and parades, accompanied by spontaneous music and dancing in the streets. The Afro-Brazilians produced their own hypnotic, pulsating sounds on drums, rattles, and sticks. Whenever a parade leader yelled, "Semba!", all the paraders would stop and dance free-style to the Afro rhythms. Eventually the command became associated with specific steps. The street scenes from the movie *Black Orpheus* will give you a vivid example of Samba music and dances.

It wasn't until the late 1920s that the uninhibited Brazilian carnival "Semba" was modified for the ballroom. The dance wasn't exactly the rage in the thirties, mainly because European and American musicians didn't know how to play Afro-Brazilian percussive instruments to create the right rhythm and mood for the dancers. By the 1940s, the Samba was a sensation. No doubt, box-office bonanza Carmen Miranda contributed considerably to the Samba's popularity.

In the sixties, the Samba's tempo was slowed down and a "Bossa Nova beat" was introduced by new Brazilian composers. The steps remain the same, only the tempo and type of sound are different.

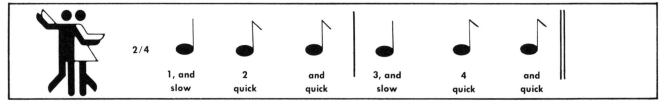

	2/4	1, and slow	2 quick	and quick	3, and slow	4 quick	and quick

or

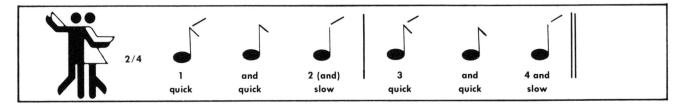

	2/4	1 quick	and quick	2 (and) slow	3 quick	and quick	4 and slow

Either rhythm applies to this dance, and other Brazilian rhythms exist. For simplicity's sake, we'll use the latter, more common, quick-quick-slow rhythm. Be sure to pause for a half-beat on the slow counts before beginning each measure. Another way of describing the footwork is "step-ball-change," or "step-close-step." Because of its style and feel, the Samba has been called the Latin Polka, but with a slight alteration in style, the basic steps are just as easily adapted to the disco floor!

SAMBA BASIC

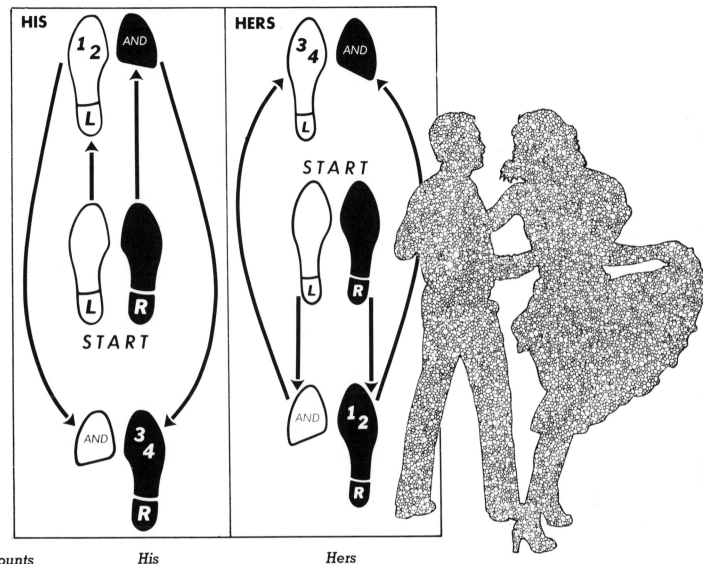

Counts	His	Hers
1	Step L forward (flat foot)	Step R backward (flat foot)
and	Half-step R next to L	Half-step L next to R
2	Step L in place	Step R in place
3	Step R backward	Step L backward
and	Half-step L next to R	Half-step R next to L
4	Step R in place	Step L in place

The knees are springing down-up-down (accent down on the first and third steps).

HOT LATIN DANCES

The Samba and Rumba share several patterns: the box step, box turn, wheel turn, balance steps, and dos-a-do. To practice the basic Samba, just flip back to the Rumba instructions for these easy patterns and apply the Samba step and style to them. Here are a few more patterns for you to play with.

COPACABANA WALK

You're both traveling forward in a one-handed break position (side by side), and you'll be using an exaggerated rocking Samba step. On the first two beats, you both step forward and swing (or swivel) outward (away from each other). On the next two beats, step forward and swing inward toward each other. In other words, you're traveling forward while you're acting like swingers at the Copa.

THE SWIVEL

This variation has the same swing to it as the Copacabana Walk, only instead of traveling forward, you're swinging in place. Start facing your partner in break position, then, using the Copacabana style, step sideways and swivel outward on the first two counts, and inward on the next two. You can swivel outward together, or you can alternate, resulting in a push-pull hand jive. Or, you can do the swivel step a few times in succession, then break one or both hands and Samba-turn in concentric circles around each other for a while. This step can be used in a myriad of patterns; just put some imagination into your feet.

EL PROGRESSO

While he's progressing forward, she's doing a cross step backward and shifting from his one side to the other. Don't forget to pause briefly for half a count on every third step you take.

Counts	His	Hers
1	Step L forward	Step R diagonally backward (toes turned in slightly)
and	Half-step R to side (toes in slightly) and swing her to your L side	Half-step-cross L behind R (toes turned in)
2	Step L in place	Step R in place
3	Step R forward and swing her to your R side	Step L diagonally backward (swing over to his other hip)
and	Half-step L to side (toes in)	Half-step-cross R behind L (toes in)
4	Step R in place	Step L in place
5-8	Repeat counts 1-4 and continue traveling	

HIS

HERS

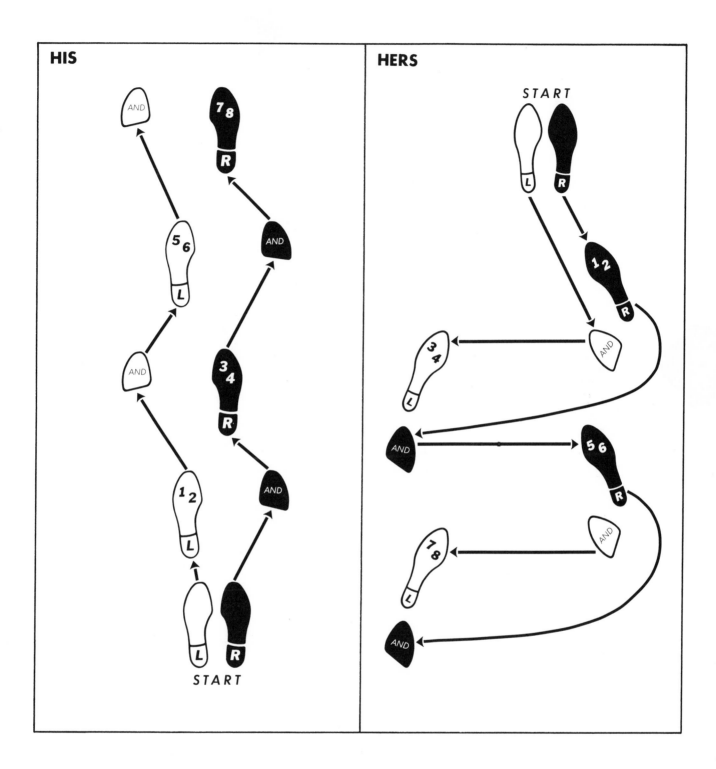

Practice this pattern until you both do it smoothly, then "progress" right into the promenade.

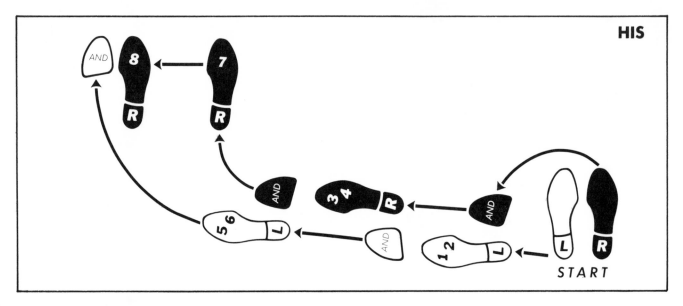

SAMBA PROMENADE

You start in closed position, immediately turn into promenade position, then end closed.

Counts	His	Hers
1	Quick ¼ turn to L (promenade position) stepping L sideways	Quick-step R sideways as you make ¼ turn R (promenade position)
and	Half-step R next to L heel	Half-step L next to R heel
2 and	Step L in place	Step R in place
3	Step R forward	Step L forward
and	Half-step L next to R heel	Half-step R next to L heel
4 and	Step R in place	Step L in place
5	Step L forward	Step R forward
and	Half-step R next to L heel	Half-step L next to R heel
6 and	Step L in place	Step R in place
7	Step R diagonally forward (into closed position)	Step L diagonally forward (into closed position)
and	Wide half-step L to L side	Wide half-step R to R side
8 and	Close R next to L	Close L next to R

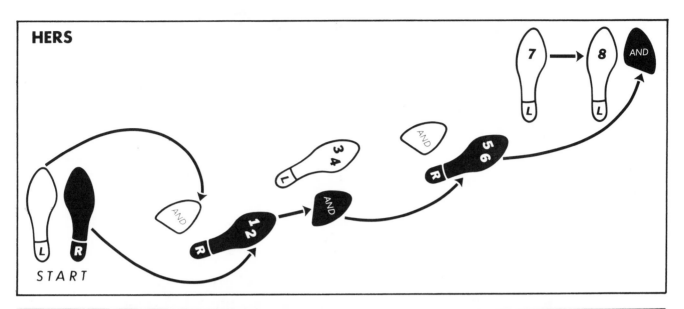

HERS

START

After you've practiced the sensual Samba styling and the simple springy steps until they're smooth, I suggest you string a succession of Samba sets together. For starters, try this:

4 basics

1 Progresso

2 basics

2 balance steps (sideways)

1 promenade

1 Copacabana Walk

2 swivels (alternate)

2 your own thing

1 box turn (L to R)

The Samba (and Rumba) are so informal that you can easily create your own racy patterns from these simple steps, as long as you maintain the individual, sensual styles of the dances. Shake it, but don't break it.

DANCE #7: MAMBO JUMBO

During the 1940s, when Americans vacationed in Havana, they danced in the casinos and nightclubs to music created by Cuban and American bands. Inevitably the musicians from both countries jammed together and Afro-Cuban rumba rhythms were mixed with the big-band jazz beat, creating what was called Mambo rhythm. The Cuban most responsible for creating the Mambo sound was Perez Prado, with his recording in the early forties of the Latin hit "Mambo Jambo." An off-beat dance evolved to synchronize with the new music. The Mambo is still the most popular dance done to Salsa music, so it is well worth your effort to learn it.

STYLE

The steps are very simple; it's the style and rhythm that may throw you. Sometimes Mambo music is played at such a furious tempo that your little feet look as if they're stepping on hot coals. As with all Latin dances, remember to keep your footwork small and tight and your knees bent and relaxed. Your upper body should be fairly still, while your happy hips are wagging horizontally.

•

The basic Mambo dance beat is an eight-count clave rhythm (named for two wooden sticks called "claves" that usually beat out the rhythm).

It looks like this:

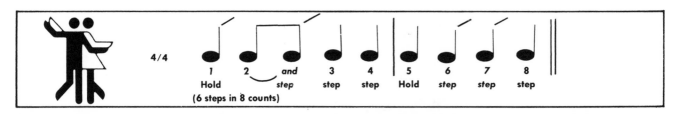

4/4

| 1 | 2 | and | 3 | 4 | 5 | 6 | 7 | 8 |
| Hold | step | step | step | step | Hold | step | step | step |

(6 steps in 8 counts)

Recommended Practice Music:
Standards: Perez Prado, Machito
Salsa: Fania Allstars, Tito Puente

The *Mambo* is called an off-beat dance because you don't accent your dance steps when the musical notes are accented. In other words, the dance rhythm is slightly different from the musical rhythm, making this a syncopated dance with a jagged rhythm. Notice that you begin dancing on the <u>second</u> count of each musical phrase (you do nothing on counts 1 and 5, just "hold"). Sometimes this is referred to as "dancing on 2." To simplify, we'll refer to the "2 and" count as just "2".

You may see a *Mambo* variation in which dancers tap or kick on the first count with the same foot that starts the second count. The steps below are written for the traditional "dance on 2" *Mambo*, but you may like to try the "tap-kick on 1" version for a change.

Take very small, flat steps and let your knees bend comfortably.

MAMBO BASIC

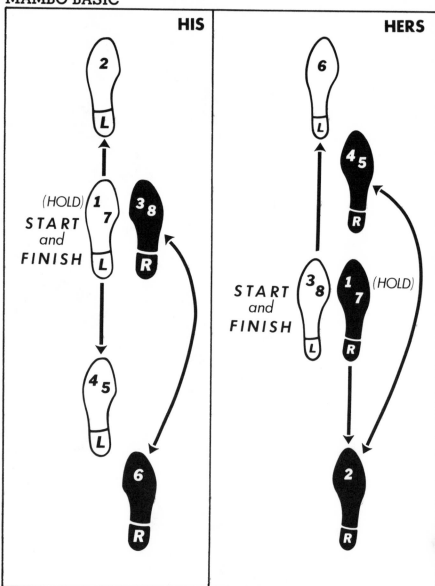

	His	*Hers*
1	Hold (feet remain together)	Hold (feet remain together)
2	Step L forward	Step R backward
3	Step R in place	Step L in place
4	Step L backward	Step R forward
5	Hold	Hold
6	Step R backward	Step L forward
7	Step L slightly forward	Step R slightly backward
8	Close R to L	Close L to R

The "hold" counts create a kind of jerky motion, typical of this dance. When you get the hang of it, release your hips and let them swing with the abandoned Salsa sounds.

MAMBO SIDE BREAK

For this variation, you both can start on the same foot, or on opposite feet; it's your choice.

Counts	His and Hers
1	Hold feet together
2	Step one foot to side (shown with opposite feet)
3	Step other foot in place
4	Close the side foot
5–8	Repeat counts 1–4, starting with the other foot

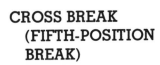

CROSS BREAK (FIFTH-POSITION BREAK)

Follow the side-break directions, only cross one foot behind the other on counts 3 and 7. You might try the cross break in open position, where you can cross one foot behind or in front of the other.

THE CROSSOVER

Start by facing your partner in break position. You may begin the crossover on either foot. If you both begin on the same foot, you'll be turning in opposite directions; if you start on opposite feet, you'll be turning in the same direction. The fun starts when you vary directions so that sometimes you're doing an opposite cross, and other times you're together. Change hands when you change directions.

Left Crossover

1   Hold (feet together)

2   Cross R over L and pivot ¼ to L on L foot all at the same time (weight on R foot)

3   Step L in place

4   Cross R next to L and face partner

5–8 R crossover (reverse counts 1–4)

THE HALF CHASE

You and your partner turn away from each other (half turn) at different times, so that you appear to be chasing each other (he goes while she comes, and vice versa), all the while doing the Mambo step in free-style position. Usually he initiates the chase after you've been dancing the basic steps a few times (although if she's inspired, she might decide to start the chase).

Counts	His	Hers
1	Hold (feet together)	
2	Step L forward	Step R backward
3	Pivot on both feet and ½ turn to R (your back is to her)	Step L in place
4	Close L to R	Step R forward
5	Hold (feet together)	
6	Step R forward	Step L forward
7	Pivot on both feet and ½ turn to L (return)	Pivot on both feet and ½ turn to R (back to him)
8	Close R to L	Close L to R
9	Hold (feet together)	
10	Step L forward	Step R forward
11	Pivot on both feet and ½ turn to R	Pivot on both feet and ½ turn to L (return)
12	Close L to R	Close R to L

This chase scene can go on and on until someone (usually he) decides to do the basic step instead of a pivot-turn. Then you'll both be left dancing the basic and thinking about a full chase.

FULL CHASE

Here you make a full turn, but not all once. You take a little break when you get halfway around. Start by doing at least one basic pattern in free-style position as preparation for this chase.

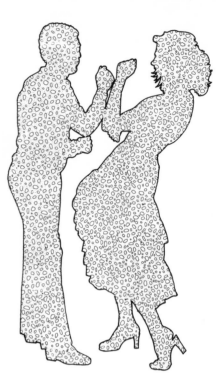

Counts	His	Hers
1	Hold (feet together)	
2	Step L forward	Step R backward
3	Pivot in both feet ½ turn to R	Step L in place
4	Close L to R	Step R forward
5	Hold (feet together)	
6	Step R backward	Follow that man (his counts 2–8)
7	Step L in place	
8	Close R to L	
9–12	Repeat counts 1–4 to finish turn	
13–16	Repeat counts 5–8	Follow his counts 2–4 (chase him and finish your turn)

The chase ends whenever one of you doesn't pivot-turn, but does a basic instead. Have fun chasing each other around.

THE CHARGE

Here's a little change of pace that's common to both the Mambo and the Cha-Cha. You and your partner charge each other sideways, but don't get too feisty about it!

Counts	Left charge:	Right charge:
1	Hold, feet together	
2	Step L sideways and thrust L shoulder toward partner	Step R sideways and thrust R shoulder toward partner
3	Step R in place	Step L in place
4	Pivot ½ turn on R and close L to R	Pivot ½ turn on L and close R to L
5	Hold, feet together	
6-8	Repeat counts 2-4 using *Right charge*	Repeat counts 2-4 using *Left charge*

A JUMBO MAMBO COMBO:

2 basics

2 side breaks

2 cross breaks

1 simple underarm turn

1 basic

2 half chases

2 full chases

2 basics

2 charges

2 basics

2 crossovers

2 your own combination

DANCE #8: HOT-CHA-CHA

The Cha-Cha is really a spinoff of the Mambo, which is itself a derivative of the Rumba. When the Mambo evolved from the Rumba in the 1940s, many Americans and Europeans vacationing in Havana had a hard time trying to dance to the racy tempo and off-beat rhythm. To accommodate the dancers, Latin-American bands slowed down the Mambo tempo from 50 to 30 bars per minute, but kept the triple Mambo staccato rhythm. In this slower version, dancers took two slow steps on the beat, followed by three steps in quick succession. Musicians would call out "cha-cha-cha" on the quickies. The heavy hip wiggles were modified to a subtle sway, and the whole affair became much more manageable for ballroom dancers. The Cha-Cha has enjoyed popularity from the 1950s right up to the present, and you occasionally see variations of it on a disco floor.

CHA-CHA STYLE:

This dance shares patterns and styling with its cousins the Rumba and Mambo. The footwork is small, flat, and close to the floor, and the knees are relaxed and a little bent, allowing the hips to move freely, but without exaggeration.

You may find this dance easier than the Mambo because you're dancing on the beat, with a little "catch" step thrown in for interest.

The dance positions vary from closed to free-style, with lots of turning and changing. places, all accomplished in a very small area. As with the Mambo, you're encouraged to invent your own steps in free-style position, using the basic Cha-Cha dance rhythm. In other words, you have an "open" invitation to be interpretive.

Recommended Practice Music
Salsa: Cal Tjader
Latin Rock: Carlos Santana
Disco: Joe Bantaan

1	2	3	and	4	5	6	7	and	8
step	step	cha-	cha-	cha	step	step	cha-	cha-	cha

(10 steps in 8 full counts)

CHA-CHA BASIC
(FORWARD/BACKWARD)
Don't forget to take small steps.

Counts	His	Hers
1	Step L forward	Step R backward
2	Step R in place	Step L in place
3 Cha	Take 3	Take 3
and Cha	baby steps backward,	baby steps forward,
4 Cha	starting on L	starting on R
5	Step R back	Step L forward
6	Step L in place	Step R in place
7 Cha	3 baby steps	3 baby steps
and Cha	forward,	backward,
8 Cha	starting on R	starting on L

OPPOSING CROSSOVER

Apply all the Mambo variations to the Cha-Cha. You and your partner can cross in the same direction, or for a change cross in opposite directions (depending upon how you feel about each other at the moment). The side break, cross break, and charge all start on the first count. For chase turns, step forward or backward on the first count, then start chasing around on the <u>second</u> count.

HOT-CHA-COMBO
Now feel free to innovate and create a few of your own Cha-Cha patterns in closed, break, or free-style positions. As long as you keep the basic "one, two, cha-cha-cha" step, you'll do just fine. Combine a few underarm turns with the footwork, string your favorite variations in succession, and you'll look hot on the Latin floor.

2 basics

2 crossovers

1 slide break

1 cross break

1 basic

1 underarm turn

1 basic

1 half chase

2 full chases

1 charge

**1 your own
hot-cha-cha thing**

HOT LATIN DANCES

DANCE #9: LEMON MERENGUE

Now, there's really no excuse. This is probably the easiest dance in the book, so be prepared to abandon all your favorite nondancer justifications. Your time has come!

The merengue arrived in the 1950s from the Caribbean, with two countries staking claims to its origins. According to the Dominican legend, a high-ranking war hero was the guest of honor at an official party. When he rose to dance, his one wounded peg leg dragged after each step taken with his good leg. The guests sympathetically emulated his limp, thus creating a new dance.

The Haitian legend describes a crippled son of a ruler who loved to dance and would drag his lame leg along the floor to the music. The courtiers, either from courtesy or demand, took to emulating the prince by dancing as though they suffered from the same affliction. Regardless of the veracity of either legend, the consensus is that this simple dance is a bit of a drag; I think you'll like it!

Merengue music is usually written in 2/4 time (most Samba and Salsa music is applicable). You'll be stepping on every beat, and accenting the first step.

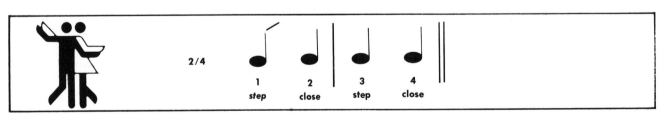

2/4

1	2	3	4
step	close	step	close

Recommended Practice Music:
Standards: Ricardo Rico
Salsa: Mongo Santamaría
Disco/Pop: *At the Copa* (Barry Manilow)

JUICY MERENGUE STYLE

On the odd-numbered counts step and dip your upper body simultaneously. (He always dips left and she always dips right on the odd counts). Bend your knee a bit when you step. On the even-numbered counts, you'll be straightening your body and sliding (dragging) the other foot to a close. By dipping, then straightening, you're creating a sideways rocking sensation, with the big dipper on the first count. At first, you'll tend to exaggerate the Merengue style and you'll feel ridiculous as you dip and limp around the room as if you were a patient in an orthopedic ward. If you prefer, you may emphasize the Cuban hip motion instead of the upper body dip. Both styles are applicable to this dance, but the photos will emphasize the dip version. Ideally, you'll be able to combine the subtle Cuban hip motion with the lame-duck limp!

Once you become comfortable with the music and style, you'll begin to refine your movements, and squeeze out the juicy essence of the Merengue for a more subtle flavor.

MERENGUE CHASSÉ (Side Basic)

You and your partner can try this in closed, promenade, or break position. Take small steps.

Counts	His	Hers
1	Step L to side and dip slightly L	Step R to side and dip R
2	Slide R close to L, then transfer weight to R	Slide L close to R, then transfer weight to L
3	Repeat count 1	Repeat count 1
4	Slide-touch R next to L	Slide-touch L next to R
5–8	Reverse direction of counts 1–4	

Practice this awhile, then move into the Dominican Walk.

DOMINICAN WALK

This is the forward-backward variation of the chassé. Try this walk in closed or break position.

Counts	His	Hers
1	Step L forward and dip over slightly	Step R backward and dip back slightly
2	Slide-close R to L and transfer weight to L	Slide-close L to R and transfer weight to R
3	Repeat count 1	Repeat count 1
4	Slide-touch R next to L	Slide-touch L next to R
5–8	Reverse direction of counts 1–4	

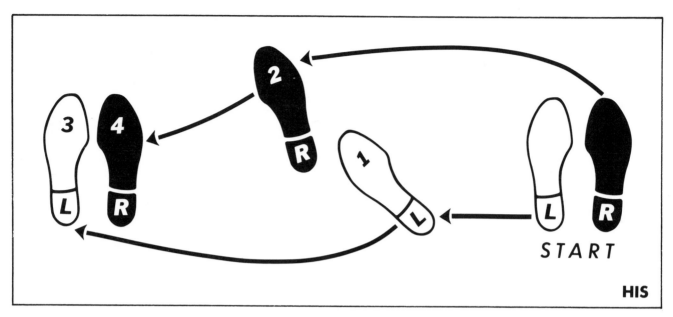

CROSS STEPS

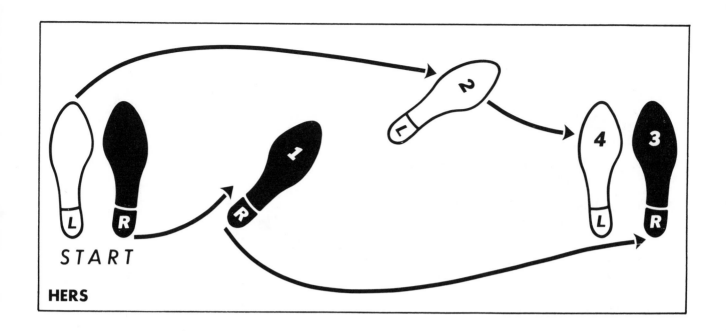

HERS

CROSS STEPS

Here you're dancing side-ways in promenade position for the first two counts, and in closed position on the next two.

Counts	His	Hers
	Step L to side (turn to prom-enade position)	Step R to side (turn to prom-enade position)
2	Cross R over L	Cross L over R
3	Step L to side (turn to closed position)	Step R to side (closed posi-tion)
4	Slide R next to L	Slide L next to R
5-7	Repeat counts 1-3	Repeat counts 1-3
8	Slide-touch R next to L	Slide-touch L next to R

Now reverse direction and re-peat counts 1-8 to the other side.

MERENGUE TURN

Partners are in one-handed break position (his left hand holding her right) and dancing concentric circles clockwise. He "limps" backward while she "limps" forward, each in a circle pattern. In other words, you're limping circles around each other.

Other turns such as the Rumba open spot turn, the simple underarm turn, the Samba dos-a-do, and the sweetheart turn are applicable to this dance, too.

MERENGUE TWIST

Try this twist in closed position: He dances the basic "step-close" in place, while twisting her from side to side on every beat. Actually she's pivoting back and forth with her feet kept fairly close together while he is twisting her with a strong push-pull arm lead. Feel free to twist her whenever you like and as often as you like, so long as you don't disengage one of her arms from its socket!

MERENGUE MIX

Once you're comfortable with the basic ingredients of the Merengue and the Samba, feel free to mix both steps into the same dance. Since the feel of the music and the rhythms of the two dances are quite similar, it is perfectly acceptable to alternate steps from each dance to the same piece of music.

In other words, try two Samba basics followed by a Merengue chassé, followed by a Samba promenade, and so on. The mixed sequence is up to you to create. Here's a Merengue combination for you to play with. Once you're comfortable with it, let loose and mix it up with sensuous Samba steps.

4 basic chassés

4 cross steps

1 full Merengue turn (8 counts)

2 Dominican Walks

4 Merengue twists

2 of your own juicy mixture

CHAPTER FOUR

DARING DISCO: TOUCH HUSTLES

Well, my terpsichorean friends, we seem to have come full circle. After spinning our way through more than two centuries of touch dancing, we've ended up right back where we started.

The disco scene today is remarkably reminiscent of earlier days of Waltz, wine, and roses. In the eighteenth century, nobility and invited guests flocked to the elegant, exclusive ballrooms throughout Europe and the United States. They became the "in" places where royalty socialized, danced, and modeled the latest fashions. Inevitably, ballrooms became so popular that paid membership was required and dress codes were imposed. The more snobbish places enforced arbitrary door controls to keep out members or guests who were out of favor with the owner. Yes, indeed, we have come full circle!

It's the same old song; history repeats itself, with a slightly different twist. Today we dance in eclectic, electric "ballrooms" to the pulsating rhythms of continuous recorded disco music. Of course, we've altered many of the original dances to suit our present style. As you'll see in this chapter, Touch Disco is really a happy marriage of something old, something new, something borrowed, and nothing blue!

DANCE #10: SIMPLE LATIN (THREE-COUNT) HUSTLE

HUSTLE HINTS

Unlike the dances in previous chapters, Touch Hustles have only one step pattern. There are no box steps, box turns, twinkles, promenade walks, and the like. There is only one basic sequence of steps. The moves are mostly sideways or forward/backward. Like the Lindy and Latin dances, Touch Hustles are done in a small area carved out on a crowded floor. The footwork is small, and when fancy turns, lifts, or dips are incorporated, the foot pattern is abandoned altogether, to be resumed after a turn sequence. In other words, the Hustle pattern is far less structured than its ancestors, in accord, no doubt, with our present free, individual, do-your-own-thing times.

Despite the fact that the three counts in this dance do not coordinate with the 4/4 timing of disco music, this dance is nonetheless performed on the disco floor. Actually, the counts and footwork appear to be taken right from counts 2–4 of the Triple Lindy or the Latin-Swing Hustle, thus its name, "Simple Latin" Hustle.

The footwork is so simple that you needn't concentrate on it. You should incorporate lots of flash from the next chapter.

The dance rhythm and musical counts match on every 4th bar. Here it is using the second variation:

Counts	His	Hers
1	Step L back	Step R back
and	Half-step R back	Half-step L back
2	Step L forward	Step R forward
3	Step R forward	Step L forward
4	Step slightly to R	Step slightly to L

Hold hands and keep repeating this basic step describing a circle. He circles counterclockwise, she circles clockwise. This basic three-count step can be done in place with turns added for interest, or in a circle pattern. When you interject continuous turns, abandon your footwork. Then pick it up again, starting with the first count.

Recommended Practice Music:
Donna Summer, Chic

VARIATION 1:

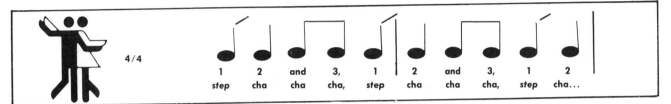

4 / 4

| 1 | 2 | and | 3, | 1 | 2 | and | 3, | 1 | 2 |
| step | cha | cha | cha, | step | cha | cha | cha, | step | cha... |

VARIATION 2:

4 / 4

| 1 | and | 2 | 3, | 1 | | and | 2 | 3, | 1 | and... |

(4 steps in 3 counts to 4-count music)

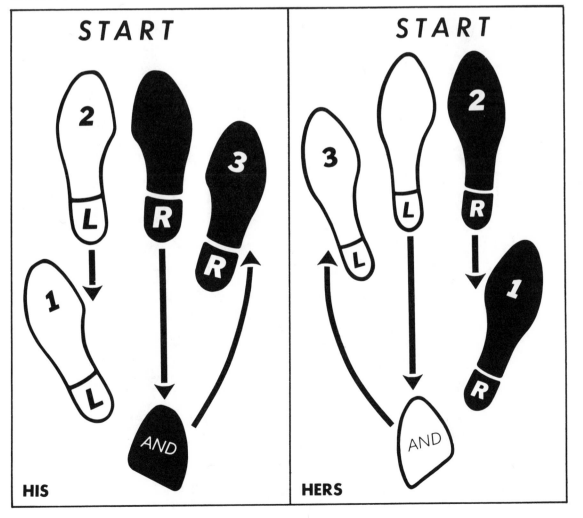

START — HIS

START — HERS

TOUCH HUSTLES

DANCE # 11: LATIN-SWING (NEW YORK) HUSTLE

The Latin Hustle has often been referred to as *the* touch dance of the 1970s. Actually, there are several variations of the Latin Hustle, the footwork differing from city to city and disco to disco. The version below is still the most popular touch dance, so it would be worth your while to learn it.If you have tried the Lindy, you'll have an easy time with this foot pattern. It is really a combination of the Double and Triple Lindy. The diagram shows this dance traveling forward and backward. Dancing sideways is even more common. In either case, be sure to take small steps.

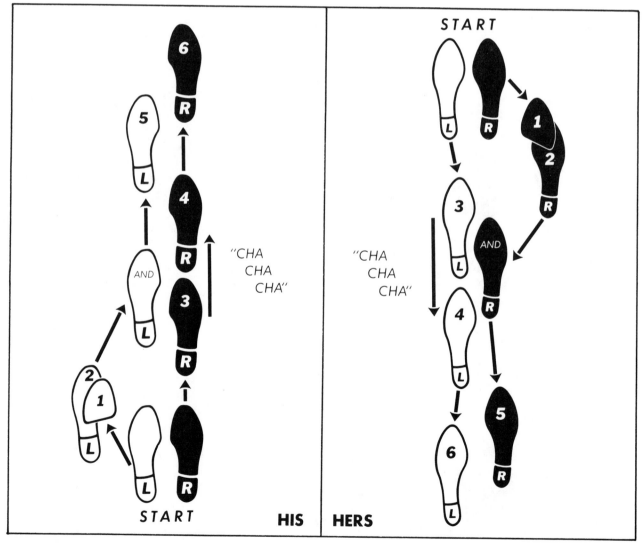

2/4

1	2	3	and	4	5	6
tap	step,	cha,	cha,	cha,	walk	walk

Counts	*His*	*Hers*
1	Tap L foot in place or slightly sideways	Tap R foot in place or slightly sideways
2	Step on L (in same place where you just tapped it)	Step on R (in same place where you just tapped it)
3	Step R 3 little "cha-cha-cha"	Step L These 3 little "cha-
and	Step L steps (or "step-ball	Step R cha-cha" steps (or
4	Step R change" in tap language) may be taken in any direction, including turning around yourself. Keep them small and nimble.	Step L "step-ball-change") may be taken in place or in any direction, including turning around yourself. Keep them small and nimble.
5	Step L two walking steps in	Step R two walking steps in
6	Step R any direction you desire; or "step, step" in place.	Step L any direction; you choose; or "step, step" in place.

Now return to count 1. Remember to practice the steps in place first, then move around with them when the footwork feels comfortable.

Now return to count 1.

Recommended Practice Music:
Santa Esmeralda

DANCE #12:   THE TANGO HUSTLE

Just as its name implies, this is another example of a recycled dance: the more dramatic, tantalizing elements were borrowed from the old Tango and updated with a few new Hustle steps. This particular combination, first popularized by the movie Saturday Night Fever, has become a favorite among couples who seek dark, secluded discos. The same sophistication and style that you gave to the Tango may be injected into this offspring.

Think sleek and stealthy.

You'll be starting in promenade position. Step on every beat.

Counts	His	Hers
1–4	Take 4 walking steps forward, starting with L	Take 4 walking steps forward, starting with R
5	Small kick on L	Small kick on R
6	Step L in place	Step R in place
7	Step R in place	Step L in place
8	Touch L next to R	Touch R next to L
9–10	Lunge forward on L	Lunge forward on R
11–12	Slide L back to R	Slide R back to L
13–16	Do a spot turn in closed position, or do a dip and any quick turn of your choice	

Repeat the entire sixteen-count sequence heading in a different direction. If you like, feel free to "throw in" a few more dips and turns at the end for four to eight more counts.

CHAPTER FIVE

HOT FLASHES: SPINS, DIPS, AND

Up to this point, I haven't discussed the delicate subject of physical conditioning. No doubt the more physically fit you are, the easier dancing will be; but to achieve skill at the dances presented here does not require any special endurance. However, when we discuss the more demanding aspects of touch dancing, such as spins, dips, and lifts, we're in a different physical league. Flashy dancing should be treated like any other contact sport; to avoid injury, you should condition for it much like an athlete during preseason training. You'll need firm stomach, thigh, and lower back muscles if you plan to recover from a dip without collapsing. You'll need flexible, strong lower back and arm muscles to accomplish lifts without dropping your partner. Resilient arm and shoulder muscles help expedite smooth spins. Unless you enjoy morning-after pain from a hearty, happy night of dancing, do try to prepare your muscles by strengthening and stretching them on a regular basis!

You'll find that it's more comfortable and natural, although not necessary, to start dips on *his* right side (dip her from right to left) and lifts on *his* left side (often coming out of a left-sided turn). Usually she turns under his left arm, although in Hustles, either arm may initiate a turn. He leads her into a turn by

LIFTS

raising one arm from a break position, and if his other arm is free, he gently pushes her waist.

With the exception of simple underarm turns, ballroom dancing doesn't call for hot flashes until the intermediate-advanced level. Disco Hustles, however, incorporate flashes in the beginning stages of learning. Certain dances use specific touches of flash. You might incorporate the Straddle Rollover into a Lindy or Hustle, but it's a bit out of character for the Waltz. Or a continuous turn sequence is popular with Hustle and Latin dances, but doesn't blend with the Tango (which favors dips). Use your own judgment and imagination, and let the feeling of the music and dance style be your guide as you ignite your own sparks. Finally, feel free to create a few flashy touches of your own as you heat up the dance floor.

SIMPLE SPINS

One good turn deserves another...and another and another. He raises one arm high from break position and turns her under it several times in succession in the same direction (which direction is unimportant). Both partners will need to abandon their footwork, and he merely "walks" around her while his raised, "turning" arm supports and spins her like a top. If his elbow is too stiff, or his grip too tight, he breaks her fingers. She is gripping only two of his fingers (not the whole hand) while she spins. This sort of spinning occurs in all touch dances, the speed and number of turns varying according to personal preference.

SWEETHEART TURN

This is a very popular turn used in Latin and Hustle dances.

Start facing each other holding crossed hands, then lift them up.

She turns under (halfway around), then scoots over to his far side so partners face the same way. There's only one way she can turn without breaking her wrists. When she's at his side, arms are bent up to shoulder height.

To cross over to the other side, she simply turns back under crossed hands. In Latin dances, this sweetheart position is accomplished by breaking hands or by starting from a one-handed break position. Try it any way it suits you best.

SPINS, DIPS, AND LIFTS

UNDERARM-BACK EXCHANGE

This is a standard Lindy turn that Hustlers also like to incorporate.

Start in a one-handed break position (hand crossed or uncrossed).

She turns under his raised arm while partners change places.

She finishes her turn while he's changing hands behind his back.

He completes the hand change, then turns to face her. The sequence is very smooth and may be repeated often, starting with either hand.

SPINS, DIPS, AND LIFTS

COMBINATION TURNS

The most innovative aspect of Touch Hustles, in particular, are the combinations of different turns strung together in succession to create a mesmerizing pretzel effect. Hustlers take pride in their original and speedy turn sequences that make them look double-jointed in the arms. Here's a typical sequence for you to start with: wrap to unwrap, to waist cross, to Holland, to spin-out. Allow plenty of bend in your elbow. Here goes!

Start in a two-handed break position (and don't break hands).

He raises one arm up and across his body for her to turn under.

He lowers the arm in front of her into a "wrap" position and scoots by her side so that partners face the same direction.

He raises the top arm to unwrap her and she does a complete turn.

She turns as far around as she can without breaking the hand position. At this point, partners are in a waist cross, facing opposite directions with one set of hands clasped at *his* belly button, and the other set of hands clasped at the back of *her* waist (the elbow must bend, or her forearm will disconnect).

From here, partners do the "Holland" (arms move as though you are balancing milk pails).

He raises the set of hands that's at his stomach up and over his neck (they go behind her waist as partners change places).

117 *SPINS, DIPS, AND LIFTS*

Partners switch places while he simultaneously raises the other set of arms from behind to in front of his stomach. In other words, partners are changing places while changing arm positions, which is accomplished by an over-the-neck arm maneuver. This tricky little double back-crossing "Holland" can have partners switching back and forth a few times in a row.

To get out of the Holland position, he raises the set of arms in front of his stomach, and instead of putting them behind his neck, he turns her out and around to face him, right where the whole sequence started.

If you manage to get through this entire twister without any casualties, without breaking your hand grip, and without pausing for a drink, then you deserve each other; stick together!

SPINS, DIPS, AND LIFTS   **118**

SIMPLE DIP

If you're looking for an easy flash on the floor, this simple dip is the answer.

You're nonchalantly dancing in closed position.

Then he twists her while he takes one wide step diagonally forward, and dips her down. To do this, he'll need to bend over a bit and lunge forward (bend knees).

She can either lift her outside knee, or for a more dramatic look, she can kick up her outside leg.

To recover, he pulls her up to the twist position, where it all started.

ELBOW DIP

For this maneuver, the guy forms a clever back brace to help her dip. It starts from any break position or turn.

He pulls her toward him and partners link elbows. His free arm is raised; her free hand is on her hip.

Moving closer together, he hooks or twists his hand so that the palm is braced against her back.

When he begins to straighten his arm downward, she dips and simultaneously lifts her outside knee. Hold the dip position a few counts, then recover. It's a sassy-looking dip when done smoothly.

DEATH DROP

A death drop is any dip that puts either partner just inches from the floor. Dipping down is no problem, it's the getting up that takes effort!

Ideally, she has strong abdominal muscles and he has strong biceps so that the effort is minimal. However, if either falls short of the ideal, remember, the secret of hoisting anything against gravity is to do it quickly. He drops her down and lifts her up *before* the momentum is lost. If you enjoy holding the position awhile, be conditioned for it!

This dip starts from a two-handed break position with either crossed or uncrossed hands.

Here it is starting from uncrossed hands (reverse the directions if starting with hands crossed).

She turns under both sets of hands, so that when she completes the turn, hands are crossed.

He whips or "pushes" her down as soon as she completes the turn.

When she feels his signal and starts to fall, she kicks up her outside leg and stops with her back parallel to the floor. Actually, the pulling tension in his arms is what stops her from hitting the floor. He'll need a strong, comfortable stance to hold her in the drop position. To recover, he sort of yanks her up while she assists by lifting herself. It helps to have a trusting relationship.

For a more dramatic drop, my partner suggests that *she* death-drop *him* occasionally!

SPINS, DIPS, AND LIFTS

SWING DIP

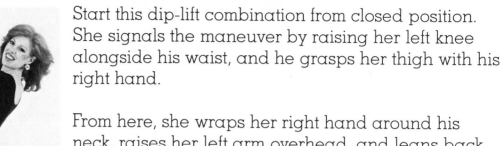

Start this dip-lift combination from closed position. She signals the maneuver by raising her left knee alongside his waist, and he grasps her thigh with his right hand.

From here, she wraps her right hand around his neck, raises her left arm overhead, and leans back. He places his left arm around her waist (are you still with me?).

She lifts off of her standing right leg, and swings it between his legs, while he dips her. To do this, he'll need to bend his knees and lean over so that she's practically sitting on his right thigh.

From here, he immediately swing-scoops her up (her right leg is still straight) and around to his right side. Then he can swing her up and center again (her right leg between his knees). This swinging up, center, up, side continues for as long as his stamina permits.

SIDESADDLE LIFT

You can jump right into this, or you may precede it with a turn, say a coil turn. It's your choice which turn you use.

As soon as she arrives at his side, he wraps one arm all around her waist (the other arm is out to the side) and lunges sideways. The knee toward her is bent, the other is straight.

She puts one arm around his shoulder (the other hand wherever she likes), and takes a quick jump, landing on his hip with her legs tucked. In order to brace her on his hip, he'll need to lean away from her slightly.

From here he may like to spin around a few times before letting her down. The higher she jumps, the easier it is for him to settle her on his hip comfortably.

SPINS, DIPS, AND LIFTS

ARABESQUE LIFT

You'll see this popular lift on the disco floor and at ballroom dance competitions. Really, it's a lot easier than it looks and reads.

Begin with a coil turn from a one-handed break position (his left hand grasping her right one).

He snaps or whips her in so that she coils around toward him. Meanwhile, he prepares his free arm for the lift.

As soon as she arrives with her back to him, she kicks her right leg up high into an arabesque and simultaneously bends her left knee in preparation for the lift. Technically, the arabesque kick would be backward, not sideways, as shown here, but the lift is easier to accomplish in the position shown.

When she kicks, he grasps her leg from under the knee, wraps his right arm around her waist, bends his knees, and lifts her. She immediately wraps her right arm around his shoulder and tucks in her left leg.

From here, he spins her around a few times, then sets her down, her left leg straightening to the floor first. This entire sequence—coil turn, arabesque, lift, spin, and let-down—all happens very quickly and smoothly without a moment's pause!

STRADDLE ROLLOVER LIFT

If there's a touch of daredevil in you, and you love to put surprises into your dancing, then you'll appreciate this flashy lift, popular from the Jitterbug era. It's actually easier than it looks here, but I'd advise you not to try it if you have a weak back or a fear of flying.

She signals the lift by bending all the way down and stretching her arms between her legs. With that signal in mind, he reaches his arms forward.

Then he stands over her, his knees bent alongside her head, and grasps her hands firmly from behind her.

With a quick, strong pull he whips her into a rollover, pulling his arms in and up.

Screaming and laughing, she does one complete roll, landing on his stomach with her legs extended straight forward, one on either side of his waist. His arms are around her waist to help anchor her in this final position. From here, partners may maneuver into another lift position of their own creation (as long as they're up there anyway), or digracefully disengage and continue to dance without pausing to think about what just happened. Good luck!

ABOUT THE AUTHOR

Karen Lustgarten is a newspaper columnist,
television personality, fitness expert, dance
and exercise instructor and consultant. Her television
segments on dance and exercise were nominated for
an Emmy Award.

Karen pioneered disco dance instruction in 1973 and
brought literally thousands of neophytes to their
dancing feet on the West Coast. She does the
research, writing, and modeling for all of her dance
and forthcoming exercise books, and for all of her
television segments.

The author resides in San Francisco and Los
Angeles, and has gained national recognition
through her best-seller, *The Complete Guide to Disco
Dancing.*